HEALING STRESS, ANXIETY AND DEPRESSION:

Magic Tricks and Guided Meditations for Stress Management. Accomplish Your Targets with Less Anxiety and Heal Your Wounds to Live Free from Depression.

Introduction

Anxiety is a feeling of worry or fear that normally apprehends you before you confront something that you consider challenging; for instance an interview, test or examination. Having such feelings is considered to be normal and a part of life. Actually, anxiety in moderation is actually good as it enables you to be focused, stay alert, and to be able to handle situations head on. The problem comes in when these feelings make you unable to sleep or otherwise function normally. This means that anxiety is seen to be out of hand when feelings such as worry or fear do not subside and continue to exist even without any particular cause or reason. This then becomes a serious condition that makes you unable to continue with your daily routine.

On the other hand, panic attacks are usually as a result of having extremely heightened anxiety. The attack might last for a few minutes or even go on for some hours but without treatment, prolonged and frequent panic attacks can be very disabling. The physical symptoms might be caused by your body getting into a fight or flight mode in response to something you assume to be a threat. Your body will therefore try to take in more oxygen and therefore your breathing will quicken. Your body will also release some hormones such as adrenaline, which will make your muscles to tense up and your heart to beat faster.

Even with the basic understanding of what anxiety is about, it is important to understand that anxiety is not just a one size fits all kind of problem; different people experience it differently. There are various types of anxiety disorders. Below are some of the most common anxiety disorders.

Panic disorder

This is a type of anxiety disorder where you experience sudden or brief attacks of intense apprehension and terror that leads to confusion, difficulty breathing, shaking, nausea, and dizziness. Other symptoms may include chest pain, sweating, a feeling of chocking and unusually strong and irregular heartbeats, which may make you to feel as though you are having a heart attack or you are going crazy. Panic attacks usually rise instantly and peak after about 10 minutes after which they may last for some hours. A panic attack frequently occurs after prolonged stress or frightening events but sometimes they might arise with no specific trigger.

BE
humble
ALL
loving
trusting
awake
aware
grateful
accepting
BE
loving
ALL
kind
grateful
aware
connected
mindful
generous
attuned
aware
awake
aware
connected
secure
BE
affectionate
grateful
attuned
aware
open
BE
peaceful
generous
aware
kind
open
BE
secure
joyful
ALL
BE
trusting
accepting
BE
ALL
BE
kind
generous
aware
BE
kind
humble
mindful
loving
open
connected
aware
awake
kind
BE
joyful
secure
BE
secure

Chapter 1 - The Best Techniques For Light To Very Intense Emotions.

Meditation tactics open up our mind to broader and more meaningful aspects of our lives that eventually lead to a happy life. Stress and happiness are inversely related; when you learn to practice meditation and become mindful of your surroundings, it reduces your stress level and creates a positive mindset to make us feel happy.

Mindfulness can be performed anywhere, anytime. The core difference between meditation and mindfulness is that meditation is done in a quiet place with your eyes closed, while mindfulness is carried out at any time as it is more about making you aware about your inner-self. Mindfulness and meditation have a similar purpose of training our thoughts to remain in the present. Mindful meditation is the term that combines both meditation and mindfulness.

There are some specific mindful meditation tactics that are quite effective in reducing our stress level and promote relaxation.

THOUGHT ACKNOWLEDGEMENT

Thought an Acknowledgement is a unique form of mindful meditation that aims to observe your thoughts and become more conscious of them. Our thoughts have an incredible impact on our minds. Our experience of reality is controlled by our thoughts. Our thoughts are powerful as they influence our behavior and feelings. Many psychological studies have proven that anxious thoughts often make us blow things out of proportion. They make things appear more daunting, bigger than they really are. A chain of negative thoughts is the worst, and that is why acknowledging and training your thoughts is very crucial to reduce stress and depression.

Mindful meditation teaches us to think about our thoughts, acknowledge them, and become more and more aware of them. We mentioned earlier about reserving judgment about our thoughts. During mindful meditation sessions or classes, guided by experts, many participants share that they cannot be able to resist external thoughts during mindfulness practice.

Mindful meditation through thought, observation is not aimed at completely blocking your thoughts or emotions, it is more about acknowledging them without passing any judgment. Allow all types of thoughts to pass by you, do not resist them as you try to raise your consciousness about your present moment. Each thought has its type and they arouse different emotions.

If you feel any emotion rising within you by a particular thought such as anxiety, happiness, stress, sadness, etc. Notice that emotion and do not pass any judgment about yourself for having that thought. Simply just move on and bring your focus back to breathing. Wait for the next thought to pass and simply repeat the observation pattern. Perceive these thoughts as powerless objects that are just floating in your mind. Notice the pattern and frequency of your thoughts.

How it reduces stress and depression?

Our thoughts are the source of all negative emotions such as anger, frustration, unhappiness, and anxiety. They create a mind trap to create a negative cycle that keeps on repeating for a prolonged time. We allow such thoughts to create a trap because we are unconscious of their effect and power. We give them permission to roam around freely in our mind to create rampant chaos. When they start creating negative emotions right after you wake up, it affects your positivity, morning energy, and creativity.

Once you are aware of this trap and unconscious thinking, you begin to change this negative cycle with the power of observation and acknowledgment. When you see yourself getting separated to these thoughts, you begin to detach from them to make them less powerful to trigger emotions.

With practice and time, you will soon begin to realize that these thoughts have no real power over you. They are just floating objects that can be easily blown away. Thought acknowledgment helps to minimize the power of these thoughts to trigger an emotional response. It helps to make you more content and at peace.

FOCUSED BREATHING

Breathing is a form of body sensation. Focuses or mindful breathing aims at improving our concentration to one particular sensation. The aim is to focus on breathing pattern, feel that sensation, and ignore other thoughts wandering in your mind.

You can indulge in mindful or focused breathing at any place, be it when you are taking a shower, making your breakfast, or going to or coming back from work in a subway. You can practice it for as much time you can allot; even 5-10 minutes of time window are adequate for one quick session. Just try to avoid too noisy or crowded places. The best way to perform focused breathing is to sit in a quiet room or garden area and practice with your eyes closed.

Start taking breathes in and out in a slow, relaxed way. Take as deep breaths as you can. The aim is to raise your consciousness about your breathing. Pick any one aspect to focus on, such as the sensation that you feel in your nose, or expansion and collapse of your chest.

Break total time that you have taken out to do mindful breathing in short windows of 5 minutes each. Now try to concentrate on your breathing and spend 5 minutes in this state of awareness.

In that 5-minute window, there will be many thoughts that will wander in your mind to pull your attention from breathing. Refrain from passing any judgment about these thoughts;

acknowledge them as just thoughts as they have come and will go soon. When that happens, break away from that thought and try to focus again on breathing.

Your mind will wander many times and that is very common. Do not feel irritated or concerned as your concentration will increase with practice and time. Remember that mindfulness and meditation aims at taking control over our thoughts and getting detached from them. Be patient while doing this. With time, you will be able to totally focus on a particular aspect of your breathing for 5 minutes. Gradually increase that time frame to 7 or 10 minutes.

How it reduces stress and depression?

Our body is highly sensitive and it is capable to experience many forms of sensations. When we have multiple tasks in mind to complete or when we feel unhappy due to any reason, it becomes hard to focus on one singular sensation. Focusing on one particular sensation helps to relax our turbulent minds. It puts at rest stressful emotions and thoughts that are troubling us.

When we feel stressed or depressed, it increases our breathing rate. It makes our breathing rapid with a shortened breathing cycle, which also increases blood pressure. Mindful breathing promotes deep and long breathing pattern to relax our mind/body and helps to normalize blood pressure and reduce stress level.

FOCUSED EATING

Focused or mindful eating is one of many tactics to improve self-consciousness and concentrate your thoughts at the moment. The aim is to focus on consuming your meal and enjoying it slowly with appreciation.

It makes you aware of various sensations associated with consuming your meal such as hunger, anticipation, food texture, taste, aroma, digestion, etc. Do not rush into it, and pick the mealtime that gives you enough space to relax and experience your food rather than just consuming it in a hurry to get rid of hunger.

Take your favorite fruit, apple, peach, mango, banana, cherry, or strawberry. Focused eating means to fully experience your food with minimal external thoughts. It helps to improve focus on your senses.

Take the fruit in your hand and feel it, with your eyes closed or open. Experience its skin texture – is it smooth, dry, soft, or little tough? Examine the fruit with your eyes, observe every detail you can, its color pattern, layers, etc. Smell it and experience its aroma, enjoy it as it comes out for a while. Eat it and feel its tastes and how it makes you feel.

You can practice this focused eating with various foods such as your whole meal, smoothie, snack, etc. to improve your concentration in that particular moment.

How it reduces stress and depression?

When we are surrounded by multiple everyday tasks or feel stressed/depressed due to any reason, it forces our mind to focus on these issues or tasks. In such an environment, we forget to appreciate small things around us that give us positive feelings and make us happy. Mindful eating helps to focus on such small things by eliminating daily concerns in that particular moment.

When you eat your food in a slow and relaxed way, it also relaxes your body and promotes better digestion. Mindful eating prevents weight gain, overeating, and reduces our stress level.

RECEPTIVE MINDFULNESS MEDITATION

We have been raised in a competitive environment that taught us that we can control everything with education, smartness, and money. We have been taught to take control of things, which often narrows our focus to many unimportant things. We mistakenly perceive our ability to control with security. When we fail to control anything, we feel insecure.

Do you feel frustrated when you fail to achieve something? Do you get angry/sad when something does not happen the way you want to? Do you feel stressed and even worse, depressed when things don't go our way. We spend hours thinking about what went wrong just to end up self-loathing.

We link our happiness to many small or big, but the particular things in life. The fact is we cannot control every single aspect of our lives and certainly not everything that surrounds us. Many times, this expectation or desire to control things about our life becomes the source of our anxiety and depression.

Our life and soul blooms when we open ourselves to experience everything and adapt a receptive attitude. Life is full of possibilities, and all it asks it to be receptive to them. A state of mindfulness teaches us to be open to our surroundings, ideas, people, opportunities, and places. It allows us to gradually get rid of the desire to control things. Let it loose and watch it blossom. You cannot control everything; no one can and it is not a healthy thing to do.

Being receptive and taking in all

Start by practicing some mindfulness techniques to open up to your surroundings and be receptive to them rather than trying to control. The aim is to not allow yourself to go ahead and anticipate the outcome. When you anticipate a particular outcome, you have already shown the desire to control the end result.

For example, if it is raining outside, focus on what rain is bringing to you. Think about all the happy memories associated with rain. Enjoy the sound of raindrops, the aroma that earth produces when those raindrops hit a dry soil surface, and the whole nature blooming around your home.

If it is not raining outside and the sun is bright and shine, dress comfortably and head outside. Do not get ahead of yourself and anticipate how you're heading out will feel or what you will experience. Do not wish to feel anything or expect anything specific from your heading out. When you do that, you are already dropping your desire to control your feelings or outcome.

Wander around and go to places that you are naturally drawn to. Take a calm, relaxed walk and make yourself comfortable. Simply be in the moment, taking in anything that you see. Be receptive to what you are experiencing at that time and open up yourself to the possibilities. It could be anything from simply watching leaves falling a tree, a cloud passing over the sun, watching a bunch of kids playing in the garden, a squirrel gathering nuts or even someone passing by you. The point is to experience stillness, sit and observe. Fully take in everything that is happening around you without making judgments.

Open up your mind to perceive life as it is, without any desire to make any changes. If anything particularly annoying or unpleasant draws your focus, such as two people verbally arguing across the street, absorb yourself in the experience as much as you are able and move on. Receptive mindfulness helps us learn how to fully take on what is going on around us by dropping your desire to control and without harboring expectations and/or judgment.

BODY MOVEMENT MINDFUL MEDITATION

Just like focused breathing, you can indulge in this form of meditation. But as we talked about meditation before, this technique involves sitting in a quiet place or lying in a comfortable position with your eyes closed. Pick a time frame when you can give your full concentration without minimal possible distractions.

Start by regulating your breathing, now gradually focus on each part of your body individually. Star feeling relaxed as you go along. For example, start focusing upon your toes and feel them getting relaxed one by one. Move on to your ankles, foot, knees, legs, etc. to arrive at the top of the head. Repeat the same process again and again.

The aim is to increase our focus by prompting our mind to concentrate on one area of the body at a time, it helps to channelize our wandering thoughts and make them focus on a particular activity. During this meditation technique, if you started feeling bored or getting disturbed by external thoughts, do not feel agitated or irritated. Accept these feelings/thoughts, continue with meditation without any judgment.

If you feel any tension around any muscle area, try to consciously relax that particular area and take a few deep breaths. It will promote muscles relaxation and improves your self-consciousness.

How it reduces stress and depression?

Body movement meditation improves self-awareness and allows us to feel small sensations that we ignore otherwise.

It promotes muscle relaxation to reduce muscle tension. Body movement meditation works in a similar way to mindful breathing to reduce stress and depression. It promotes relaxation, normalizes blood pressure, and reduces stress level.

GRATITUDE MINDFUL MEDITATION

When our mind is filled with chaotic, rampant thoughts right after we get out of bed in the morning, the thought of being grateful towards life never comes into thought. Starting your day with the practice of being grateful is one great habit to start. Mindfulness is also about being aware of the things we have in the present and be grateful for them.

For example, when you open a fridge to get eggs to make breakfast, you don't feel gratitude for having enough eggs. It is probably a very small to you, but it is a cause of great concern to someone who does not have any money to buy food. Being grateful should not be mistaken as settling for anything. You can wish to earn a six-digit salary, a luxurious home, an expensive car, and so on, but you can still be grateful for making enough money to have eggs in your fridge.

This is one example, focused on your financial aspect. The same thing applies to many other aspects of your life, including your job satisfaction, career planning, relationships, family, health, and so on.

Being optimist is great, it's good to make progress in your life and achieve your dream goal; however, all of this can be achieved in the midst of being grateful. Showing gratitude is one of the most well-known aspects of Buddhist monks. They begin the day with a chant of gratitude that their life offered. Each and everything that you have or own is nothing but a blessing, no matter how small or big.

The monks in Tiber, make prayers every morning for all the sufferings they have experienced. When these monks can be grateful for their sufferings, why can't we be grateful for the things we possess right now?

Practice it in your routine. It is not about how much time you spend every day and how many things you can feel gratitude for. It is about being mindful of your surroundings and immersing yourself in a state where you can feel deeply blessed.

How it reduces stress and depression?

Gratitude can be shown to many big and small blessings of our life. We overlook these blessings in the midst of our chaotic life. Gratitude mindfulness provides positive feelings to our mind to prevent it from focusing on everyday challenges and frustrations. It grounds us at the moment and raises our self-consciousness.

Research studies have narrated the link between well-being and gratitude. Showing gratitude is known to reduce anxiety, depression and promotes the feeling of fulfillment. It improves sleep quality, relationships, and boosts self-esteem.

SLOWING DOWN WITH MINDFUL MEDITATION

If you have noticed by now, nothing in the world of meditation and mindfulness is done in a hurry or in a rushed state. The society around us puts high significance on work being in done quickly. Speed and productivity have become integrated words in our modern social dictionary. Slowing down might give you a feeling of giving up on training skills or your best efforts.

Mindful meditation teaches to slow down for a moment and take another look at the thing you want to accomplish. Slow down for a while and ask yourself "Is rushing into this thing is the only way to accomplish it?" You will be surprised to guess that answer by yourself as you will realize that you can accomplish that thing without rushing into it.

In many cases, rushing into things has resulted in producing low-quality results, which could have been successfully completed, otherwise, be it a work project, dishwashing, cooking meals, driving somewhere, and so on. If anyone or anything is making you rush into doing anything, try and stop it. If you have no option but to finish that task in a hurry, then do it and focus on other tasks that you can do at your willful speed.

How it reduces stress and depression?

When you rush yourself from one task to another all day long, it not only makes you physically and mentally exhausted, but it also takes away a sense of accomplishment. Rushing for things is associated with an increase in our blood pressure. When you are completing a task or feeling rushed to achieve something in a hurry, it increases your stress and anxiety.

The key is to make a conscious effort to slow things down instead of racing to tick off tasks from your list. Remember, excellence always wins over speed. Learn to say no to things that can cause interruption. Concentrate all your energy in doing the job is the best possible way.

That is where the ability to focus and placing all your concentration in your present moment comes into practice. Calm yourself, focus all your attention to a task at hand, be mindful about only that task at that moment, experience it, enjoy working on it and work on successfully completing it without any rush. It makes you relaxed from within, improves your concentration level, and gives you a feeling of accomplishment.

MINDFUL MEDITATION WITH POSITIVE AFFIRMATION

Mindful meditation clears clutter in your mind to make way for positive affirmations. Positive affirmations are the backbone of your confidence, positive body language, and self-development. They are nothing but a by-product of positive thinking. They create positive changes in your lifestyle, be it your financial concerns, relationships, and many other things you are passionate about.

Positive affirmations can be in the form of encouraging or disparaging words. They are positive phrases that describe who you are, what are your values, and/or what you want to achieve/become. They have the power to change the structure and functions of our brains.

Positive affirmations are countless and vary from one person to another. These affirmations need to have constantly chattered in your mind as many times in a day as you like. They can be anything that you truly wish to change something about your life; it can be very specific or very general. Following are some examples of positive affirmations.

I always can. I will.

I am forever brave I am fearless.

I believe in my experience

I am and deserve to win

I will clear that test in the top 5%

I will score more than 92% in my final exams.

I am who and I can be who I want to be.

I have great internal strength to cope with any challenge.

Mindful meditation aims to imbibe positive affirmations in your mind with continuous repetition. It motivates you to act upon these affirmations to achieve your goals. When you get up in the morning and think about "I will lose 2 pounds in this month, or I am not afraid to be wrong". How long do you think this will keep you motivated? Maybe 2 hours or 24 hours?

Do not take this wrong, there is nothing wrong with thinking positive and telling yourself. However, the reason for being unable to keep yourself motivated by that particular sentence is constant chattering of thoughts in our unconscious mind. Positive affirmations have a great impact on you when you are in solitude, away from chattering of thoughts. That is why mindful meditation as a concept aims at calming your mind and being conscious.

Indulge in mindful meditation practice covered in this book for at least 10-15 minutes, it will put your mind in a calm, receptive and conscious state. Feel relaxed and tune in with your inner feelings, and then chant positive affirmations. Your affirmations are now energized and will have a great capacity to motivate you to fulfill them.

FINDING HAPPINESS WITH MINDFUL MEDITATION

A permanent cure for a common cold is still not been discovered yet, despite unbelievable advancements in the field of medical science. Does that mean we drop our weapons, and accept defeat? What it reflects is that we all have our limitations, no matter who you are. The solution to every problem is not resolving the issue, but to manage it in a smart way.

The very existence of human beings till date proves that it has given the greatest gift of unbeatable spirit to rise from any adverse situation. Just like the common cold, the reasons for anxiety and depression are countless. However, what it takes is to adopt a mature approach to identify them, analyze them, and fight back at them by learning to meditate and achieve a true state of mindfulness.

No matter how bad, turn your life has taken, there is nothing that meditation and mindfulness cannot resolve. They are the most effective sources to achieve great wisdom and inner peace. Mindful meditation takes time to get into it and feel its effect. Being patient is the key here. Make a routine to practice the mindful meditation tactics covered in the book to gain inner consciousness, and find a true source of your inner happiness by remaining in the moment.

Chapter 2 - A Breathing Technique To Help Combat Insomnia.

There is an assortment of relaxation techniques systems to look over. Successful completion of relaxation techniques for longer time provides benefits which help us in increasing level of productivity and ability to relax, including the improvement of a positive energy. The benefits are multifold-reduced muscle tension, along these lines, lessening the body's requirement for oxygen and decreasing exhaustion and uneasiness.

Focus on Breathing

If you find that stress is causing you to lose your sleep, this relaxation technique can be sought. Focusing on breath, would help you to relax your mind and reduce worries and stress. Since deep breathes infuse more oxygen in your bloodstream, profound breathing helps you unwind. If you are doing it for the first time, there could be some difficulty but eventually your body will get used to it.

To enable yourself to concentrate on your breathing, it is better to find a solitary, empty space. Dim light conditions are preferable as they help soothe our mood. This isn't at all mandatory to follow this rule; however, it can enable you to concentrate on the training in case you are amateurs.

Locate an agreeable, calm spot to sit or rest

Take your place

Sit straight and relaxed

Take a moment to get comfortable

Don't do anything

Just sit completely relaxed for a few minutes

Make sure there is nothing disturbing you

Now, close your eyes

Then put your one hand on our lower midsection

Breath normally

Keep your focus on your breathing

Inhale, and watch the air travel through your body

Exhale and let the air take away all your thoughts and negativity

Inhale

Exhale

Take a long slow, deep breath in

And slowly exhale

Attempt to take a whole breath so your lungs are full

Feel the air coming in through your nose move descending, extending your lungs completely and your lower midsection rises

Inhale out through your mouth

Take another deep breath in

And exhale

Repeat few times more

Breathe in

Breathe out

Breathe in

You are becoming very relaxed

Breathe out

Release all tension and stress

Breathe in

With each breath the air infuses calmness

Breathe out

Feel the air leaving your body conveys strain, worries and stress with it

Now put one hand just underneath our belly button

Loosen up your stomach muscles

Inhale

Exhale

As you continue with the deep breathing

Feel your hand rise a little (and fall as you exhale)

Inhale

Exhale

Your chest rises marginally, as well, working together with your midriff

Inhale

Exhale

As you breathe out gradually, it would be more relaxing to allow any sound made by your throat come out

You must not hold back

Use the chanting word would "Om" to help you

Utter these words as you exhale

Take a deep breath in

Now exhale: "Oooooommm"

Again, take a deep breath in

And exhale: "Oooooommm"

If any distracting thought occurs

Don't worry about it, it may happen

Use the "Oooooommm" word to find your focus

Take a deep breath in

Now exhale: "Oooooommm"

Again, take a deep breath in

And exhale: "Oooooommm"

Now start breathing normally

Stabilize your breathing

Let it return to its normal rate

Remain seated with your eyes closed

Try to feel your surrounding

You are feeling completely relaxed now

There is no worries, anxiety, or stress

You are very calm

You can open your eyes.

Deep Breathing

Deep breathing is a simple method to unwind and release your stresses. Likewise called belly breathing, diaphragmatic breathing, and stomach breathing, it can bring down your pulse and loosen up tense muscles. It can enable you to wash away a portion of the worry of your day and get ready for a more settled, more loosening up night. Pick a period that works for you. Attempt to keep a similar everyday practice once a day to pick up the most advantage out of it.

You can do it essentially anyplace, and it just takes a couple of minutes. In case you're fatigued and don't have 10 minutes to de-stress, even a couple of full breaths can help. When you've drilled it a couple of times, a small-scale variant of this activity can help ease stress. Simply envision that every breath is clearing ceaselessly pressure, and you may quiet your uneasiness in one moment or two.

When you figure out how to profound inhale, you can utilize it to quiet you anyplace. When you're sitting at your work area or doing work around the house, know about your breathing and the pressure you are feeling. Keep in mind your profound breathing everyday practice and let the pressure blur away. Utilize this bit by bit manual for figure out how to overwhelm your stress.

Locate an agreeable, calm spot to sit or rests

Pick a spot where you realize you won't be aggravated

Take your place

Stay calm and relaxed

Take a moment to get comfortable

Don't do anything

Just stay completely relaxed for a few minutes

Make sure there is nothing disturbing you

Notice if there is tension anywhere

If you feel any part tense, release the tension

Adjust your body to release the pressure

On the off chance that sitting, keep your back straight and your feet level on the floor

Now, close your eyes

Start by breathing normally

Inhale

Exhale

Don't try to increase or decrease the rate of your breathing

Just focus on your breathing

Inhale

Exhale

Put one hand on your midsection, just underneath your ribs

Focus as the hand on your midsection goes in with the breath

Take a deep breath through your nose

1...2...3...4

Make sure your chest does not rise while your stomach expands

Holding your breath

Breathe out through your mouth

4...3...2...1

Do this practice multiple times until you have a quieting beat

Inhale gradually through your nose

1...2...3...4

Holding your breath

Gradually exhale through your mouth

4...3...2...1

Inhale

As you breathe in, envision that the air you're breathing is spreading unwinding sensation all through your body

Holding your breath

Exhale

As you breathe out, envision that your breath is whooshing ceaselessly stress and strain

Repeat this process a few more times

Breathe in

1...2...3...4

Hold your breath in the abdomen

Exhale through your mouth

4...3...2...1

Breathe in

Every inhaling is energizing

Hold your breath

Exhale through your mouth

Every exhaling is calming and relaxing

Breathe in

1...2...3...4

Hold your breath in the abdomen

Exhale through your mouth

4...3...2...1

Breathe in

1...2...3...4

Hold your breath in the abdomen

Exhale through your mouth

4...3...2...1

Now stabilize your breath

Feel how relaxed you are

All the stress was released

Your mind is calm and clear

You are in a perfect harmony

Take this feeling with you

Now open your eyes.

Roll Breathing

Roll breathing causes you to grow full utilization of your lungs and to concentrate on your relaxing. You can do it in any position. Yet, while you are learning, it is ideal to lie on your back with your knees bowed.

Practice move breathing day by day for a little while until you can do it anyplace. You can utilize it as a moment unwinding apparatus whenever you need one. Some individuals get tipsy the initial couple of times they attempt move relaxing. In the event that you start to inhale excessively quick or feel woozy, slow your relaxing. Get up gradually.

Locate an agreeable, calm spot to sit or rests

Pick a spot where you realize you won't be aggravated

Lie on your back

Bow your knees

Stay calm and relaxed

Take a moment to get comfortable

Don't do anything

Just stay completely relaxed for a few minutes

Make sure there is nothing disturbing you

Notice if there is tension anywhere

If you feel any part tense, release the tension

Adjust your body to release the pressure

Now, close your eyes

Start by breathing normally

Inhale

Exhale

Do not rush the process

Just focus on your breathing

Inhale

Exhale

1

Put your left hand on your tummy and your right hand on your chest

Notice how your hands move as you are breathing in and out

2

Work on filling your belly by breathing so that your left hand goes up when you breathe in and your right hand on the chest stays still

Continuously take in through your nose

Now add the second means to your breathing

Breathe in first into your belly as in the past

And after that keep breathing in into your upper chest

Inhale gradually and routinely

As you do as such

Your right hand will rise

And your left hand will fall a little as your tummy falls

4

Now inhale out the air first from your belly

And only then from your chest

Notice how at first your left hand

And afterward your right hand fall

As you breathe out gradually through your mouth

Make calm, whooshing sound

Repeat these 6 to 8 times

Inhale gradually with your belly

Then inhale slowly with your chest

Now exhale gradually with your belly

Then exhale slowly with your chest

Notice that the development of your belly and chest rises and falls

Like the movement of moving waves

As you breathe in,

Notice the energy flowing your body

As you become full of vitality

As you breathe out

Feel the strain leaving your body

As you become increasingly loose

Inhale gradually with your belly

Then inhale slowly with your chest

Now exhale gradually with your belly

Then exhale slowly with your chest

Inhale gradually with your belly

Then inhale slowly with your chest

Now exhale gradually with your belly

Then exhale slowly with your chest

Inhale gradually with your belly

Then inhale slowly with your chest

Now exhale gradually with your belly

Then exhale slowly with your chest

Inhale gradually with your belly

Then inhale slowly with your chest

Now exhale gradually with your belly

Then exhale slowly with your chest

Now bring your breathing back to normal

Remain lying for a while

Became aware of everything in and around you

Now open your eyes.

Box Breathing

One of the simplest and best breath work procedures is box breathing. No, this doesn't include sitting in one of those goliath boxes you get when you move to another house, yet rather alludes to the example itself. Known to be highly effective in promoting peaceful sleep, Box breathing includes giving equivalent time to a nasal breathe in, first breath hold, nasal breathe out, and second breath hold. The rhythm and cadence of box breathing makes it relax. It urges us to concentrate on tallying the corner of each of the four "sides."

Since the in breath and outbreath are equivalent, this method adjusts to your sensory system and help you simply settle and bring your body and mind back to the focus. Box breathing is ideal for relaxing, especially when one of its advantages include promoting-sleep.

Box breathing is an extraordinary procedure for us to deal with everyday stressors as well. The system works in a wide range of stressful circumstances. Hence, it is recommended for everyone. Except children younger than 7-8 years of age, this procedure can be advantageous to anybody, particularly the individuals who need to think or reducing stress.

It is recommended to attempt to rehearse box breathing technique for 10 to 20 minutes on a daily basis, ideally simultaneously of day. On the off chance that that target appears to be unattainable, you may attempt it for a couple of minutes at whatever point you feel and stop it when you become uncomfortable. On the off chance that you practice this technique at list for 5 minutes daily you will see a huge effect in your everyday life.

Locate an agreeable, calm spot to sit or rest

Take your place

Stay calm and relaxed

Take a moment to get comfortable

Don't do anything

Just stay completely relaxed for a few minutes

Make sure there is nothing disturbing you

Notice if there is tension anywhere

If you feel any part tense, release the tension

Adjust your body to release the pressure

Now, close your eyes

1

Inhale through your nose while counting to four gradually

1...2...3...4

Feel the air enter your lungs

2

Hold your breath inside while counting gradually to four

1...2...3...4

Make an effort not to clasp your mouth or nose shut

Basically, abstain from breathing in or breathing out for 4 seconds

3

Start to gradually breathe out for 4 seconds

4...3...2...1

Rehash stages 1 to 3 in any event for 4 minutes, or until calmness returns

1

Inhale through your nose while counting to four gradually

1...2...3...4

Feel the air enter your lungs

2

Hold your breath inside while counting gradually to four

1...2...3...4

Try not to clasp your mouth or nose shut

Basically, abstain from breathing in or breathing out for 4 seconds

3

Start to gradually breathe out for 4 seconds

4...3...2...1

Let's repeat again

1

Inhale through your nose while counting to four gradually

1...2...3...4

Feel the air enter your lungs.

2

Hold your breath inside while counting gradually to four

1...2...3...4

Make an effort not to clasp your mouth or nose shut

Basically, abstain from breathing in or breathing out for 4 seconds

3

Start to gradually breathe out for 4 seconds

4...3...2...1

You are doing great

You are feeling completely relaxed

There is no fear now

There is no anxiety

There is no stress

You can open your eyes now

Or choose to stay in this position for a bit longer

Relish the feeling for as long as you want.

Chapter 3 - Practices And Routines To Develop A Balanced Life From Every Point Of View.

"But if you can create an honorable livelihood, where you take your skills and use them and you earn a living from it, it gives you a sense of freedom and allows you to balance your life the way you want."

— Anita Roddick

"When you have balance in your life, work becomes an entirely different experience. There is a passion that moves you to a whole new level of fulfillment and gratitude, and that's when you can do your best . . . for yourself and for others."

—Cara Delevingne

"Work is a four-letter word." What do you think of when you hear the word "work"? How does it make you feel? Brainstorm the words that come to mind and write them down. What do you notice? Is your list full of positive words or negative? Does the word "career" conjure up different feelings and ideas?

I find it sad that statistics show the vast majority of people worldwide are dissatisfied with their jobs. In an article in Forbes Magazine, "Unhappy Employees Outnumber Happy Ones by Two to One Worldwide," Susan Adams gives information from a massive report by the Gallup University. Gallup gathered information from 230,000 full-time and part-time workers in 142 countries. They found that 87% of workers worldwide "are emotionally disconnected from their workplaces and less likely to be productive." They said that "the U.S. has some of the best numbers in the world, with 30% happy in their work, 52% feeling blah and 18% who hate their jobs." I won't go into all the reasons but Gallup put together a list of twelve statements regarding employee engagement. Four of them stand out as they relate to this book and the topic of balance:

"At work, I have the opportunity to do what I do best every day."

"The mission or purpose of my company makes me feel my job is important."

"I have a best friend at work."

"This last year, I have had opportunities at work to learn and grow."

When I consider the topic of balance, especially between home and work, there are some key components that can help you to strike that balance and to feel more content. The Gallup statement about having the "opportunity to do what I do best every day" is often overlooked by employers, which causes workers to feel dissatisfied and disengaged. I can't begin to count the number of times I have worked with clients who have had this complaint. They were hired for a position they were excited about—where they excelled. When they did well in that position, they were promoted out of it to something that didn't use their strengths, and frankly, wasn't interesting to them. When employers don't use their employees' skills, strengths and interests, everybody loses in the happiness and productivity departments.

I had a client who had worked as an airplane mechanic for many years. He was so good at his job that he was given a promotion, one that his spouse urged him to accept because it offered a higher salary. He took it and became depressed as he didn't feel like he was able to use his skills and interests. He had a lot more paperwork, had to get training in project management, and felt a lot less confident in his skills and abilities. He no longer enjoyed work as he had in the past. When a mechanic position opened, I encouraged him to check it out to see if it was more in line with his strengths and if it would provide more job satisfaction. He became excited about it, talked it over with his spouse, and took the position. He immediately felt more balanced in his work and home lives because he was using his hands-on strengths at work, which reduced his stress and improved his home life. His story illustrates why it's key to know your strengths and to find a position where you can use them. So-called promotions are not necessarily going to give you any more work satisfaction (other than maybe a higher paycheck), so it is important to be true to yourself when offered a "better" position.

I have had several similar work experiences. The one that pushed me over the edge was my last position in the school system where I was hired as a social skills teacher instead of as a school counselor. I felt sorely underused. Although I enjoyed the students, I didn't get satisfaction from supervising lunch. I wanted to use my education, my skills, training, and strengths to the fullest and this position didn't meet those needs. So I quit one month before school dismissed for the summer, and I began working as a counselor in the private sector, where I could use my strengths, skills, and education.

EXERCISE 1: Write about a personal experience you have had where your strengths and skills were underutilized or not used at all. How did you feel about that position? How did you feel about your employer? What did you wish would have happened in that situation?

____

____

____

____

____

____

____

Let's look at the second statement in the Gallup study: "The mission or purpose of my company makes me feel my job is important." Do you feel like your job is important? Do you know what your company's mission is? Do you feel like your position contributes to that mission? Many people go through life seeing their job as a paycheck instead of a purpose, but work and home life will be out of balance if your values don't align with those of your company. For example, if being conscientious about the environment and recycling is important to you, but not to your employer and you witness a lot of waste at work, you may find it difficult to work for this company. You may choose to bring it to your employer's attention and work on a solution that aligns more with your values. If the employer doesn't see the value in your suggestion, you may find it difficult to stay.

EXERCISE 2: What are your current employer's mission and values? Do they match your own? What would it take for you to find meaning or purpose in your current position?

Take some time to evaluate this.

____

____

____

____

____

____

The third area in the Gallup survey is: "I have a best friend at work." You may have heard about a "work spouse," which could be a best friend at work or someone you work closely with on a daily basis. Many people find at least one close friend at work, someone who is in a similar position or works in the same area. Colleagues you enjoy are extremely important to your work satisfaction and to your work balance. If you don't make connections with others at work, you will likely be unhappy and move on. Why would you want to stay in a job where you don't feel a connection to your coworkers?

EXERCISE 3: Who is your best friend at work? Do you feel connected to your co-workers? Have you ever left a job because you didn't feel

connected to your colleagues? Write about it.

____

____

____

____

____

____

____

____

The fourth thing that stood out from the Gallup survey was: "This last year, I have had opportunities at work to learn and grow." Have you felt stagnant at work? Have you been in a place where day after day, it seems like the same old thing? No challenges, nothing new to learn. When boredom sets in, workers become less productive. Some employers require training, but it isn't always pertinent to everyone's position. For example, when I was a school counselor, I spent two days in math training that was required for all educators in the school district, regardless of whether or not we would use it. This can be just as frustrating as having no training at all. I much preferred training that was useful to my position.

EXERCISE 4: Have you had opportunities to learn and grow at work over the past year? Describe them.

Did you attend job related training in the past year? Was the training useful to you? Did it help you do your work better? How did you feel about the training? Were there other opportunities you wish your employer would have provided? Did you make suggestions to your employer about future learning opportunities? If so, what were they?

____

____

____

____

____

____

____

____

EXERCISE 5: If you have a vision of the perfect position for you, describe it here. What aspects are essential to your enjoyment at work?

____

____

____

____

____

What about creativity at work? Even if you aren't an artist or musician, creativity can still be part of your work. Creativity comes in lots of sizes, shapes and colors and can be as simple as finding a new way to do something or looking at a problem in new ways. If you work on an assembly line and there is a certain way that everything must be done, you may feel like you can't be creative. But what if that isn't really the case? What if you could find a new way to accomplish the same task? Maybe it is a minor detail in the way that a tool is used or the way the line is set up. Maybe you have an idea on how to make work more fun, keeping coworkers engaged and helping everyone to be more productive. Problem solving is creative and can make the job run smoother for yourself and others.

EXERCISE 6: How can you make work more creative or fun? Look at some of the smallest things you could do. Maybe there are ideas you have about rearranging the space to be more efficient, or maybe there are steps that could be simplified to make the job easier. Think about it and come up with at least one idea. Consider proposing it to

your boss.

Effective Planning

Many clients have come to me over the years feeling stressed because they don't feel like they plan effectively. This causes them to be less productive and sometimes leads to issues with their supervisors. We work on some simple strategies to help manage time and plan effectively. I recommend they follow five steps to effective planning.

The first step is to prioritize the tasks that need to be done. What tasks are urgent and have a looming deadline? Which tasks are important? Which ones are both important and urgent, and which ones are neither urgent nor important? Use the table in the following exercise to determine where you should be focusing your energy.

EXERCISE 7: Make a list of all the tasks that need to be done, then place them in this table according to their urgency and importance. This is an easy way to prioritize your day and to decide what really needs to be done. This also makes it easy to see which things are not important so you can delegate, dump or do them later. List your

tasks to be done here:

____

____

____

____

____

____

____

____

____

____

Now place them in the grid according to their importance and urgency.

	IMPORTANT	NOT IMPORTANT
URGENT		
NOT URGENT		

Something that is often overlooked is your energy level. The second step is to consider your high energy and low energy times and use them to your advantage. Schedule the most challenging tasks during your high energy time and save the least important tasks and the ones that don't require as much effort for the low energy times. Mornings are my high energy time. The problem is that I want to do everything in the morning: exercising, writing this book, taking classes or workshops, and seeing clients. I must prioritize which of these things needs to be done the next day and work the others in around the most urgent and important. My low energy time is afternoon, around 3:00 to 5:00 p.m. I use this time to check email, do my billing, make phone calls, tidy up, and run errands. Sometimes I see clients during this time as it works with their schedules, but I prefer to see them earlier so they get the more energized me.

EXERCISE 8: Take some time to figure out your high energy times and low energy times and write them here. Use this information as you plan how you use your time tomorrow. If you aren't sure when you are at your best, pay attention to your energy levels over the next week and record what you learn on the calendar provided.

____

____

____

____

____

____

____

____

The third step in effective planning is to eliminate distractions. This is difficult to do in this high tech, fast-paced world where we've been trained like Pavlov's dogs to respond to every ding or ringtone from our cell phones or computers. Carve out some time to turn off the distractions. I know this sounds radical, but phones do have an "off" button. If shutting off your phone completely sounds too stressful, at least turn off the sounds and vibrations so you can give yourself the gift of freedom from distractions for a few hours. Do you remember what that is like?

Schedule a block of time when you don't respond to calls, colleagues or emails. If you have a door, close it. Post a sign letting coworkers know when you'll be available. Schedule the time you will respond to coworkers, emails, text messages and phone calls. You will be amazed what you can accomplish if you do this. Discipline yourself to stick to this schedule. According to an article in the New York Times, entitled "Brain, Interrupted. Does distraction matter — do interruptions make us dumber?", every time you have to stop and start a task due to distractions, it takes 20-30 minutes to get back to where you left off. If you add this up throughout a day, you will be amazed at how much time is wasted due to distractions!

EXERCISE 9: Keeping in mind your high and low energy cycles as well as the distractions that pull you away from the work you want to complete, make a plan for your day which blocks out high energy times for you to be productive and work without distractions. Set aside this time daily and notice how much your stress is reduced and how much more you accomplish. Here is a calendar to get you started. Make changes to customize it for your schedule.

Time Management Chart			
Time	Sunday	Monday	Tuesday
6-7 a.m.			
7-8 a.m.			
8-9 a.m.			
9-10 a.m.			
10-11 a.m.			
11a.m.- 12 p.m.			
12-1 p.m.			
1-2 p.m.			
2-3 p.m.			
3-4 p.m.			
4-5 p.m.			
5-6 p.m.			
6-7 p.m.			
7-8 p.m.			
8-9 p.m.			
9-10 p.m.			
10-11 p.m.			
11p.m.-12 a.m.			

Time Management Chart			
Wednesday	Thursday	Friday	Saturday

The fourth step to consider in planning effectively is to set time limits. It is too easy to get bogged down with tasks that aren't urgent or important. When you set time limits on these tasks, you will feel more in control and will save yourself time and energy for tasks that are important and urgent. As I mentioned previously in the section on eliminating distractions, instead of responding to every email as it comes in, change your settings so you don't receive notifications until you are ready to deal with the email. Then stick to a time frame that allows you to respond in a timely manner and get back to the next important item on your list. When you schedule time to respond to email or phone calls, set a timer so you don't get trapped into giving away your most valuable, productive time. I suggest checking email twice a day, once in the morning and once in the afternoon. Notice how much more you accomplish when you don't have to stop and start repeatedly.

An important part of keeping your work life balanced is to complete what you set out to do within the time frame of the work day. Leave your work at work at the end of the work day. Give yourself a true break when you leave the office so you are refreshed and ready to get back to work in the morning. When you set time limits, you are in control and you set yourself up for success!

The fifth step is to plan at the end of the work day what you want to get done the following day. By doing this, you set the ball in motion to accomplish tasks that otherwise wouldn't get done when they need to be done. I do this every night. I write my list in my planner. (Yes, I do this the old-fashioned way instead of on a computer, but you can do it in whatever way is useful to you.) I have found that I accomplish a lot more this way, than if I wait and create the list in the morning. It is easy to forget my train of thought from the day before. Make a list of the top three to five tasks that need to accomplished the next day and carve out the time to get them done. Use your table of urgent and important tasks to help you prioritize. Be sure to schedule these tasks during the time frames that best fit the energy level required. When you arrive at work in the morning, you will be amazed at how much more efficient and productive you are as a result of planning the day before!

EXERCISE 10: Try planning tomorrow's work at the end of each work day. Make this a five-day experiment. Check off each day you accomplish this, then record how you felt.

Day 1 ☐   Day 2 ☐   Day 3 ☐   Day 4 ☐   Day 5 ☐

____

____

____

____

____

____

____

____

____

The only point I will make is that if you get involved in these types of activities to build business and to meet people, you may find that this is one aspect that offers more fun to your work. As Mary Poppins says, every job was a bit of fun. When you find that fun—SNAP! The job's done!

When you are having fun, your life feels more balanced.

Finding Financial Balance

This is quite possibly the area of our lives that causes the most stress, most conflict, and most concern. Most people spend an inordinate amount of time focusing on money. Have you noticed how many times a day you think about money? What are your first thoughts? "Should I be spending this money? Do we have enough in the account? What will my partner say when they see what I have spent? What if I lose my job? How will we pay the bills? Maybe I should get a second job to cover the remodeling project. I don't think we can afford to go on vacation this year.

The kids need new clothes and shoes. How much will that cost?" You can quickly find yourself in a self-talk money spiral and the theme will most likely be "Is there ever enough money?"

Growing up I often heard:

"Time is money."

"Money doesn't grow on trees."

"A penny saved is a penny earned."

There is truth in these sayings, but there is also a feeling of scarcity or fear. As a child, I remember hearing adults say that wealthy people were more concerned about money than those without much. The premise was that the more people had, the more they had to lose so they spent much of their time trying to protect their assets. This seemed to be a rationale for not trying to accumulate wealth. As an adult, I've often wondered how life in a town with a population of 830 would have been different if the common belief had been one of abundance instead of scarcity.

In my growing-up family, scarcity was the fear and the reality. My dad spent money on Winston cigarettes and Tvrsky's Strawberry Vodka which left little for food and clothing for four children. Add my sister's illness into the mix and there was even less. Gram bought back-to-school shoes, snow boots and winter coats for us. Mom bought material on clearance and made our clothes when we were young. Later, when she was working two jobs, she had another woman in town make them for us. We wore them until they were ragged and our pants were above our ankles. We were on food stamps and grew a large garden. Mom and Gram canned corn, beans, beets, pickles and anything else they grew so we had food throughout the winter months. Much of our meat came from hunting or fishing. Going out to eat was a treat and didn't occur very often.

Our house was the second oldest one in town and in need of repairs that my parents couldn't afford. The green and white checkerboard linoleum floor in the dining room was peeling up as was the speckled linoleum kitchen floor. The front porch had rotting boards. The house and window trim was peeling and needed to be painted. Mom wanted to have a nice home, but the best we could do was to keep it clean, so every Saturday we cleaned it from top to bottom, including dusting every book on every shelf of our rickety black metal bookcase. We had one bathroom for six people and we shared beds and bedrooms. When I was in junior high, we got a small window air conditioner. We fought over who got to stand in front of it when we came in after being out in the 100-degree summer heat. We couldn't afford to run it all the time, so it was only turned on in extreme cases.

My mom was the one who paid the bills and managed the checkbook. There was constant stress and anxiety about finances and how the bills were going to get paid. Gram helped Mom to pay the bills, unbeknownst to Dad. He was deep into his addictions and Mom was left to figure it out. She stashed five dollars here and there to buy us some clothes, or saved for a rare vacation like the time we went to Kansas City to Worlds of Fun and a Royals baseball game for a day. I don't know how she paid for doctor's appointments. I think most of the time we just didn't go and relied on Gram who was a registered nurse for our medical care. I didn't know that people were supposed to get their teeth cleaned regularly because the only time we went to the dentist was when we were in pain. Dad's overspending caught up with them and he was forced to sell the variety store he had bought from his parents. I don't know how they managed to avoid bankruptcy, but it was close. Dad talked about saving but I didn't see it in action. If it hadn't been for Gram saving money and leaving some inheritance, my parents wouldn't have had anything for retirement. As I look at my growing-up family and how they viewed money as a scarcity, I see how it impacted me. I was a saver from the first time I was given money for Christmas or my birthday. When I began earning babysitting money in fifth grade, I saved it in a hand-me-down wallet and hid it in my bedroom. There was no allowance. We all earned our own money. In seventh grade, I started working as a janitor at the school, sweeping floors and dumping trash after school. My brothers and I worked as janitors at the school in the summers, too. We worked from 7 a.m. to 4 p.m. with a one-hour lunch break. I saved as much as I could every summer.

I paid for my clothes, school activities and entertainment. I didn't splurge on things that I didn't think were necessary. (Once I did splurge on a pair of platform shoes for the junior high prom and quickly regretted it when they began falling apart shortly after I bought them.) I bought my own car. My dad picked out the 1973 Vega Station Wagon. I then went to the local dealership and wrote the check for $750.

To this day, I am a saver. I love seeing my account balances grow, especially my investments! As I write this, I am still the proud owner and primary driver of our 20-year old Plymouth Grand Voyager minivan! Why? Because it is a reliable vehicle, is very comfortable and I hate making car payments. I know I can't drive it forever, but I know its quirks (certain door locks don't work anymore, etc.) and I hate to let it go as long as it is running fine. We could afford a new vehicle and have even test-driven some, but I keep asking "is it necessary?" Amazing how old programming continues, even when we are aware of it!

Security is important to me and I don't want to live in a constant state of fear of not having enough money like my parents did. I learned to squirrel away money like my mom, so I have money ready for the trip to Hawaii that I'm planning to take with my friend Jen. It gives me peace of mind to know that I could go today if I wanted to, and I wouldn't have to worry about how I was going to pay for it. Although Hawaii isn't a necessity, it is a splurge that I am looking forward to. As I evaluate the ways I spend money, I see that I value experiences. I would much rather go to Hawaii or on another nice vacation than spend money on a new car. As much as I love to save and invest money, I also want to enjoy the present, which is, after all, a gift. If we save everything and don't enjoy spending some of it now on having fun, we may miss out and never get to enjoy the fruits of our labor! Quinn likes to travel, too, so we take vacations every year. We have other friends who don't enjoy traveling so they splurge on local entertainment such as concerts and sporting events. It is up to each of us to determine how to balance the spending between necessities and pleasure.

Clients often show up in my office due to financial stress. Unfortunately, if they have too much financial stress, they discontinue after working with me for only a short time. I understand this and encourage them to take care of their financial health. If they are stressed about paying me, they are not going to enjoy it and they won't get as much out of it. I want our time to be helpful, fun and productive so I want them to take care of themselves. After all, that is what I teach them. If paying for sessions with me could add to their financial stress, we sometimes schedule appointments further apart or make them shorter. I also remind them that it is a matter of priorities and that sometimes they must choose between their mental and emotional health (coming to me for coaching or counseling) and giving up something else (a bad habit such as smoking, for example). It is amazing how people can find money when there is something they really want! I have occasionally been burned by a client who claims financial hardship so they delay paying me, and later I find out they spent an exorbitant amount of money on Christmas gifts or they went on an extravagant vacation or they roll into my parking lot with a brand new vehicle. This becomes a point of discussion about values, priorities and responsibilities. We work on connecting the dots so they can see that it is this very behavior that is causing them financial stress and will continue to do so as long as they continue to spend in this way.

It is very difficult for some people to discipline themselves to spend responsibly. The examples that are set by politicians, celebrities, and our government are not the best examples to follow. Look at our national debt and the unwillingness to deal with paying it off. Many people feel entitled to have what they want whether or not they can afford it. The attitude seems to be, "Why not? The government spends when they don't have the money so why shouldn't I?" Our society is a fast food, click on a button and give-it-to-me-now society and people don't want to delay gratification. Our world has become impatient and people think that rewards should come immediately and without any effort. People don't want to exercise self-control because it isn't as much fun as getting what you want right now. There are so many problems with this attitude that it is hard to cover it in a short space, but I will do my best.

When you find yourself acting out like a child and thinking, "I don't care if I don't have the money. I want it now!!" it is time to step out of the child part of yourself and step into the grownup part of yourself. In therapy, it is called Transactional Analysis or T.A. for short. The basic theory is that we all act from one of three parts of ourselves:

the parent

the child or

the adult.

When you want to have a tantrum because you want something now, you are acting out of your child part. Think of children who want the candy near the checkout at the grocery store. They don't think about it and plan ahead to buy it, but it is all they can think about when they see it at eye level. This is impulse buying and businesses strategically design their checkout lanes to sell to people who are thinking short-term and want immediate gratification. It works or they wouldn't do it. Children are not known for their money smarts (remember Jack and the magic beans?), so when you get in child mode, you will not be making the best financial decisions.

The parent in these situations is the one who tries to reign in the child by telling him or her "NO! You can't have it, ever!" The problem with this is that when the prospect of all fun is taken away, the child will act out and rebel against the new rule.

Chapter 4 - Working With Symptoms

Listening To Your Body; Working With Emotional Pain

Instructors and doctors often advise you to listen to your body. Whether you are trying a new exercise routine or a diet plan, you are supposed to interpret the signals your body sends and choose between the alternatives accordingly. It is the first step towards a healthy life, as they say. So, what are these messages your body is trying to convey and how can you effectively use them?

Body Talks

Everybody has its limitations. Many people injure themselves and make things worse by obsessing over exercising. If they have laid out a routine to exercise for 30 minutes straight, they will continue to do so even if their bodies are screaming for help. Ignoring this call can prove to be a big mistake; your body very subtly tells you what it wants and how you can avoid any harm coming your way before it manifests, you just need to hear closely. In case you have acute pain in your body, it is better to give it a rest and try not to injure yourself. Regardless of what others may be doing, you need to listen only to your body and compete with yourself. You can modify your exercise plan as per your body - work out for 30 seconds, take 30 seconds rest and then proceed to the next exercise. Eventually, you would be able to exercise without resting much, but it will take time...

However, pain is also part and parcel of a workout. Because when you start your workout, your body is stiff - it takes time and consistency to adapt to the change to the new exercise lifestyle and gives you pain, to some extent. Although your body aches, your muscles function fully, and the pain is more in your head than in your body. These are the times when you start finding reasons to get away from the workout and everything else is better than exercise. Don't underestimate yourself - your body is made to survive, to be pushed to its limits. Persistence and hard work will pay off - they will make you fit and stronger, and your body will be better guarded against the diseases.

Exercise helps you in being aware of your body and its movement. It develops a deep mind and body connection which will only help you to understand yourself and your body better in the long run. The only thing that is required is, to be honest with yourself. Starving is not the answer - dieting takes away the energy your body needs to function because the food is fuel for the body. Eat when your body suggests you are hungry and eat until you're full. Go ahead when your body gives a green signal and stop or slow down when it doesn't. Remember, your health and happiness depends on the harmony between your body, mind, and soul. Once you're aware of what you're body desires, you will lead a content, healthy and fit life.

Listen to Your Body, Or it Will Shout Louder

Our bodies have a way of communicating with us. They may give us pain, tiredness, an itch, or indigestion. All these are signals given by our bodies to get our attention to fix the underlying problem. These signals are often misinterpreted as annoyances though. And it is sometimes hard to discern when we have a real problem and when we do not.

Take for example someone with a very bad toothache. They can take something to dull the pain, but that pain is there for a reason. They may need urgent dental treatment. If they continue to ignore the pain, they may require hospitalization. And some tooth and gum germs have been linked to conditions such as heart disease, so a toothache is not something to be dulled or ignored.

And anyone who has suffered a broken arm or leg will tell you how terrible the pain was. This is because the body is saying that we must get help. The body keeps asking for this help until we seek it and fix the problem.

Sometimes, however, the warning signs are more of an insistent whisper than a loud scream. For example, asthma, eczema, an unusual bump or lump, and so on. In this case, we should seek medical help and also do everything we can to help ourselves to better health. For example, someone who experiences tiredness may be warned by their doctor that they have the first signs of diabetes. As well as taking their doctor's advice, they can also make changes to their diet and exercise to reverse or control the condition before it takes hold.

And now and then I get a client with a physical manifestation like Chronic Fatigue Syndrome or Multiple Chemical Sensitivities that want to work and play way over what their bodies can cope with. Such a condition is just the body talking to its owner, and if the owner does not listen and slow down, the body will resort to shouting. Sometimes people want to eat junk food and take no exercise. Other people may wish to under-eat and over-exercise to be thin. And then they wonder why they feel ill or get the disease. And it is easy to wonder. Our modern-day culture discourages holistic thinking. And it is common for people to be unaware of how to live holistically.

All is not lost though. And there is no better time than the present. Maybe we can all take a few minutes out of our busy schedule and ask ourselves how we can listen better to our bodies today. And whatever revelations come to us can show us a way forward. Then we can have a dialogue with our bodies. And this leads to better understanding and co-operation. So, what do you think your body is telling you today?

Workout Tip - Learn to Listen to Your Body

Nowadays, there are a hundred and one ways to track and measure all kinds of body-stats. Almost everyone you meet in a gym has a heart-rate monitor and a professionally planned workout-log, at the very least. Not that they always use them, but they have them...

In all this, it's easy to forget that your body still gives you the most subtle and most important kind of feedback before, during and after your workouts. In particular, it tells how far you can push yourself.

Many people make the mistake of either never approaching their limits or pushing themselves too hard. There are two types of people: Those who tend to be "lazy" and those who tend to over-do it.

If you belong to the "lazy" category, then you probably quickly find excuses for not working out today or for not pushing yourself. You may have planned to do three sets, but you're only doing one because of some reason or other.

If you're an over-doer, on the other hand, you probably have "tough guy syndrome". You feel like you need to be tough and that suffering is just a part of progress. You feel like you couldn't forgive yourself for skipping a workout and you have a lot of negative self-talk that pops into your head at any sign of weakness or laziness.

In both cases, you need two things:

1. Someone who can tell you which type you are.

The problem is that we can't ourselves tell which type we tend to be. You need someone who can objectively and truthfully tell you which type you are. Ask a friend or your trainer and believe their answer.

2. Learn to distinguish between two types of pain.

Pain is a part of working out, to a certain extent. However, there are two different kinds of pain. There's the kind of pain that's worse in your head than in your body. The kind of pain that makes you want to stop because sitting on a couch is more comfortable than doing another repetition. The kind where your muscles burn but still work.

Then there's the "deep pain." This is the kind that goes beyond just a burning sensation and should not be ignored. This is the kind of pain where your body is truly telling you to take it down a notch and give yourself some rest.

If you've been exercising for a while, I have no doubt you know about both these types of pain. The key is, to be honest with yourself. Don't be a tough-guy and try to push past the "deep pain." That will only get you injured (believe me, I've made my fair share of stupid mistakes like this...). On the other hand, don't be a wuss and stop training before you've reached your limits. Burning muscles are part of the deal.

It comes down to being honest with yourself and being conscious of what's going on. Pay attention and learn to listen to your body. You'll make more progress this way, that's for sure.

Chapter 5 - Mood Changes

Anxiety and negative thoughts go hand in hand. Your anxious thoughts are likely rooted in negative thoughts that were never challenged along the way, and when those negative thoughts go unchecked, they lead to negative feelings, which lead to negative thoughts. Those negative feelings are pervasive and infectious; they have a way of spreading to all sorts of other thoughts, slowly corrupting your own thought processes so you are largely thinking in negatives rather than positives, which can be detrimental to your life as a whole. People avoid those whose minds are rooted in negativity—they do not want to be infected themselves. Those who are negative become difficult to tolerate, especially because most people tend to orient themselves with positive thinking. Therefore, those who are negative often find themselves largely rejected by those around them, which really only exacerbates the negative thoughts.

Defining Negative Automatic Thoughts

Negative thoughts, at least for the purpose of this book, are more specific than just any thoughts that are negative. We are specifically discussing thoughts that are automatic and pervasive, that color your behaviors and understandings of those around you. Your negative thoughts are going to be the automatic thoughts that are responsible for guiding your behavior so you do not have to think about it.

We all have automatic thoughts—these are thoughts that save your conscious mind from spending precious real estate, figuring out what to do next. For example, you likely do not consciously think about your reaction to slow down and stop when a light turns red when you are driving—you just do it. You have developed the automatic thought that tells you to stop driving when the light turns red. This is a good thing because if you had to consciously think about each and every aspect of driving, it would be incredibly tedious, exhausting, and difficult. You would suffer if your child bickering in the back seat with a sibling caused you to lose the focus necessary to drive effectively. However, sometimes, those automatic thoughts that you have learned become negative—they begin to encourage you to behave negatively because the thoughts themselves have been corrupted. You may have negative automatic thoughts that tell you that you are undeserving of any real, healthy relationships. Without you being aware of it, you likely were constantly behaving in ways that were negative. You were engaging in behaviors that were negative and when the negative consequence happened as a result, you used it as justification for the negative thought.

Identifying Negative Thoughts

When you need to identify your negative thoughts, the best way to do so is engaging in self-reflection or journaling. When you do this, you are essentially parsing through your thoughts, trying to understand what the root of the thoughts you are having are. When you get to the root of a thought process, you identify the negative thought that you were having. That negative root is responsible for everything that came after it, and when you know what it is, you can begin to directly counter that root and make it a point to clear it up. When you engage in this process, you are essentially going to repeatedly ask yourself why something matters to you or why it is important or what it means to you, depending on which makes the most sense in that particular context. When you finally get to a statement that is something about yourself, such as, "I am unlovable," or "I am broken," or some other thought that is a direct description of yourself, you have arrived at the negative automatic thought you are holding about the situation.

The first step to doing so is to identify problematic behavior or feeling. Stop for a moment and think about the last time that you felt incredibly negatively. Perhaps you were trying to talk to someone else and the other person turned you down instead. You then felt incredibly upset. Deciding to focus on that, you stop and consider what that feeling of upset meant in the first place. Why does being told no upset you so much?

After careful contemplation, you decide that being told no was upsetting because it made you feel as though the other person did not actually like you. You are convinced that the other person not liking you is the exact reason you were told no. Now, you need to ask yourself why you think the other person does not like you.

Again, considering your answer carefully, you eventually decide that the other person does not like you because no one could ever like you. You are sure of that because you are unlikable in general. Now, you are once again going to ask yourself why that is the case and try to identify what it is about the situation that makes you unlikable.

You answer that you are incapable of doing anything right. Again, ask yourself why that is the case or what that says about you. You are almost there now!

This time, your answer is that you are incompetent in general. Finally, you got to the root automatic thought. It is directly about yourself, describing something you believe to be true about yourself.

Some people prefer to reach this point through journaling, stopping, and deciding that they want to create a direct record of their thought processes. Some people are simply visual learners, and through applying the visual process in front of them, they are able to begin to notice patterns over time as they continue to unearth automatic thoughts.

Others do this through self-reflection and mindfulness, focusing on letting their thoughts flow rather than writing anything down. This is okay, too, if it works for you; but, after the fact, you should make it a point to write down the negative thought so you have it in mind for the future.

When you finally have your automatic thoughts identified, it is time to start identifying which are negative thoughts. The negative thoughts are like the weeds in your mental garden—you want to remove them before they can spread and destroy all of the healthy, good, wanted plants. When identifying which thoughts are positive and healthy or negative, you must cross-check each of the thoughts against a list of negative thought patterns.

Common Negative Thought Patterns

Ultimately, there are 15 negative thought patterns that are largely common. These are the most likely patterns that your thoughts will take if they are negative, and because they are the most common, they will be the best starting point. Keep in mind, however, sometimes a thought will somehow miss all of these points but still be problematic or negative. For this reason, use the list provided as a guideline rather than as some definitive list.

Filtering

When you engage in filtering, you look at only the negative, rejecting the positive that has happened around you as well. You refuse to acknowledge the good, turning a blind eye to it and in doing so, you develop an incredibly pessimistic view of life. For example, if you got an 88% on a test, you are likely to focus on the 12% that you got wrong rather than seeing that you got 88% of it correct. You see that 12% as a flaw and feel as though you should have gotten 100%.

Polarized Thinking

Also known as black and white thinking, this is closely related to filtering. When you engage in polarized thinking, you refuse to acknowledge that there is plenty between perfect and failed. You think that anything that is not exactly perfect is a failure, despite the fact that perfection is unattainable. For example, you assume that the entire meal you cooked was an utter failure because the rice you made was just barely undercooked. Instead of recognizing that the rest of the food was delicious, you dump everything and deem it a failure and instead order a pizza.

Overgeneralization

When you engage in overgeneralization, you are essentially taking one or two instances of something happening and applying that as a rule you use to determine future interactions or predictions. For example, you may decide that all of your past relationships failed, so this one will as well. In that instance, you are essentially dooming your current relationship to failure even though that might be the one.

Jumping to Conclusions

This negative thought pattern involves you assuming you know exactly what will happen next before it actually does happen, even if you have no real reason that can justify your thoughts. You assume that you will fail that test you have coming up because you are bad at the subject, so you do not bother studying for it at all. Of course, jumping to that conclusion basically guarantees it, then, because you fail after refusing to study.

Worst Case Scenario

When you think in terms of the worst-case scenario, you assume that the worst will happen, even though there are several other much more mundane, less disastrous explanations. For example, when your child misses your phone call, you assume that he was kidnapped and sold into human trafficking instead of assuming that his battery died or he forgot to turn the volume on his ringer after school.

Personalization

When you engage in personalization, you are essentially assuming that you are the root cause of any suffering around you. If you see someone at the grocery store that looks annoyed, it has to be your fault. If you see someone having a bad day at work, you think that it must be caused by your own behavior or failure to provide the care necessary.

Control Fallacy

When this is your negative thought pattern, you essentially give yourself far more credit for influencing those around you than is actually true, to more of an extent than is present in personalization. In this case, it is your fault that there was an accident outside your house last night because you forgot to change your lightbulb, so it kept flickering outside, and the flickering was enough of a distraction that it caused an accident.

Fairness Fallacy

When your thinking falls for the trap of the fairness fallacy, you are essentially hyper-focusing on fairness. You assume that everything must be fair, whether it is the case or not. When life is not fair, you assume that you have been wronged and therefore focus on that fact, emphasizing that you should have gotten the same as the other person. This, of course, keeps you hyper-focused on the past and ideals rather than looking at skills, personality differences, or the million other ways someone else might be more deserving of something than you.

Blame

When you engage in blaming, you are either blaming outward or inward in a way to explain away the behavior. You may assign blame to yourself, focusing on the fact that it is your fault that something happened for reasons that you may not be able to totally explain rationally, or you may blame someone else to avoid blaming yourself, such as saying that the reason you failed your latest exam was because you were sick and therefore not in the right mindset.

Should Haves

When you focus too much on the should-haves, you lose track of the fact that many things in life do not play out the way they should. Parents should not lose children, but it happens. Focusing on what should have happened is essentially just keeping your mind focused in the past rather than allowing yourself to recognize the fact that things do not always work exactly as planned.

Emotional Reasoning

Think about the words involved in the naming of this negative thought pattern—emotional and reasoning. They are exact opposites. When you are using emotional reasoning, you are using your emotions to rationalize your thoughts. Essentially, you decide that your feelings are accurate and allow them to color your thinking. For example, if you feel like you failed, then you will call yourself a failure.

Change Fallacy

When you use this sort of negative thinking, you assume that other people will or have to change for you in some way, and when they do not change for you at all, you lose focus on what the reality of the situation is. You get so caught up in the fact that other people need to do things for you that you stop trying to do things for yourself.

Labeling

Labeling refers to assuming that something can be reduced down to one or two words. For example, you label yourself a failure because you have messed up, or you label a job you have as pointless because you feel like you cannot get anywhere. You fail to see everything else that whatever you are labeling actually is and reduce it down to the simplest terms possible.

Refusal to Admit Wrongdoing

When you engage in this sort of thinking, you essentially reject the possibility of being anything other than right. Even when someone provides you with concrete evidence about whatever has happened or contradicting your claims, you assume that it is wrong altogether. There is absolutely no possible way you can be wrong, even if you have to twist things in order to have even a possibility of being right.

Heaven's Reward

When you fall for Heaven's reward thinking, you assume that your good deeds must be rewarded. If you do something good for someone else, you feel like you have to get some sort of benefit for it, despite the fact that in the real world, no one cares to reward you for doing what is expected of you or what makes you a good person.

Chapter 6 - Meditation

Effective meditation is one of the most powerful tools for reducing anxiety and panic. Meditation refers to a group of exercises that involve someone sitting down and focusing on something such as their breath or an object. Meditation has several benefits that help alleviate anxiety symptoms.

To begin with, research shows that meditation can help someone gain control of their physical tension by generating a calm reaction. During meditation, the heart rate slows down which in turn reduces blood pressure, and when repeated often it can make people feel less anxious and better able to cope with their anxiety.

Meditation has been known to drastically increase a person's ability to control anxious thoughts that trigger panic by teaching you alternative ways to respond to your anxious feelings and worry. Therefore, instead of you dwelling on your negative emotions and fear and letting them control how you respond to situations, you learn how to control your feelings and respond positively to stressful situations.

When we panic, we let the irrational thoughts and emotions that we are feeling control the way we respond to the situation. We make small problems appear bigger and insurmountable, and small decisions become life and death decisions. We focus so much on the problem and our ability to solve it to the point we cannot even remember what caused the problem. The reaction triggers panic, which is what our brain will remember to associate similar situations with, so the next time we are in similar situation, our brain responds by sending our body messages that induce similar panic every time. By meditating, we are learning to take control of our thoughts, to disassociate ourselves briefly with your thoughts so that we can better analyze them later instead of being consumed with the thoughts. Your brain now no longer registers the panicked response; instead, it registers the calm, relaxed response so the next time you are faced with a stressful situation, your brain sends the message to your body to relax and calm down.

Meditation teaches you to calm your mind and slow down your racing thoughts, and to tune in to more positive reinforcement which in turn helps improve your cognitive and learning skills. As you continue to practice meditation, you will start to notice that you are able to focus better and rein in irrational thoughts. If you master meditation, you will be able to notice when your mind wanders off during class or work meetings and be able to rein your thoughts back to the appropriate thing you are supposed to be focusing on.

Meditation can help people suffering from anxiety attacks learn how to let go of control, especially in certain situations where they are surrounded by circumstances beyond their control that trigger their anxiety. For example, as you are preparing to leave your home for the office, you receive a phone call from a friend telling you that your company is going to be laying off staff. The phone call disrupts your routine and you leave the house five minutes later than you planned, and as you reach the bus stop you find that the bus was early today and that the next bus is going to be coming in the next thirty minutes, which means you will be late to work.

Your natural response is to panic. You have just heard that your company is lying off people, you wonder if you are now one of them and you will not have a job, which will make you unable to pay rent, which will make your landlord evict you, and then you will have to live in the streets. Your thoughts have made you blow the situation out of proportion, which induces more panic that makes you unable to handle the situation. If you are someone who regularly practices meditation, you will realize after you miss the bus that you have other options. You can call someone and see if they will be able to drop you, or you can call your boss and explain that you are running a few minutes late. You realize that you can remain calm even if you are stuck in a bad situation.

To start meditating, look for a quiet place where you will not be disturbed or easily distracted. Focus all your thoughts on one object or word; you can also choose just a sound such as "mmh" and gently repeat that word or sound for around twenty minutes. Some people find it beneficial to use their breathing pattern as something they can focus on for the stipulated twenty minutes. Basically, in meditation, what you are doing is quieting your mind and allowing it to focus on one thing at a time. This process of meditation can help you learn how to process your thoughts when you panic. For instance, when you are called to give a presentation at school or at the office and your thoughts tell you that people will laugh at what you will say, or that you are not adequately prepared, then you reinforce those thoughts by seeing yourself fainting or forgetting everything. Notice that by this time your thoughts and feeling are out of sync with the reality — nobody has heard your presentation so how can they think it's stupid? To gain control of our emotions, we need to learn to distract ourselves from negative thoughts.

Chapter 7 - Creating A Stress-Free Environment

Let's be clear. In this section, I'm not talking about a stress-free physical location. Some of these exist, yes, but not many. The goal here is to discuss steps you can take to help your mind feel less stress. Your brain is what produces stress hormones that then run rampant and lead to fight-or-flight chaos. If you can do specific things to help calm your mind, your environment will naturally feel that much less stressful. Granted, sometimes you may have to change physical locations in order to help your amygdalae relax. It all depends on your particular needs.

Emphasize Communication

Specific individuals may be stressing you out, or they have the power to help you address another stressor (such as an HR rep who can help you with a coworker you feel uncomfortable around). When discussing it, think of the word talk and not complain. Take time to reflect on what is stressing you specifically. Identify what you personally can and cannot change. Then take steps to communicate the situation. Keeping quiet may feel safe but it's the worst thing you can do for your stress level. The conflict will just continue to bubble and boil inside you until it finally bursts out in some kind of nasty altercation.

Set aside time in a neutral location (where neither of you will feel like you're on the other person's "turf") to talk about the problem. Use "I feel/because" statements rather than "You did this" or "It's your fault." So, "I felt angry when you contradicted me in front of the children today because we didn't present a united front" versus "You make me so mad when you don't agree with me in front of the kids!" Be specific about the situation that upset you.

Then present a possible solution, "It would be helpful to me if, when I discipline Bob at the dining room table, you don't disagree immediately. If you have concerns, please address them with me afterwards, in private, and I'll make sure to listen and consider taking a different approach next time."

You can use this approach with any kind of relationship. "I feel/because," followed by a clear solution. If the person you're talking to doesn't like the solution, that's okay. You may not resolve the conflict immediately. The fact that you are communicating and starting to address an issue—and you continue to communicate until the problem is resolved and thereafter to ensure other problems don't arise—will be a huge factor in creating a stress-free mental environment.

Prioritize Time for Yourself

Wait. Didn't you see this one already in the previous section? Yes. That's because it bears repeating. The more you set aside specific time for your physical, mental, and emotional health, the more stress-free your environment will be. While you may not love exercising, going for a regular walk will help you from head to toe, including your mood and stress level.

Prioritizing time for yourself can involve regularly scheduling a clean-up of your personal space. If you have files all over the place at work, your stress level is going to be high because you'll probably lose things. Seeing so many files will also remind you of how many tasks remain unresolved. So, make keeping your personal space neat, uncluttered, and comfortable a priority.

Schedule regular time to meet with friends or family. This isn't a luxury. It's absolutely vital to your mental health and stress level.

Regular checkups are also a part of prioritizing time for yourself. Don't skip a doctor's appointment because you're overwhelmed with work. You are more important than work. You only have one body and one brain. Once damaged, you can't replace them. Take care of yourself, inside and out.

Remove Yourself from the Situation

Easier said than done, right? But sometimes, it's vital. If your work environment is toxic to the point where you simply can't fix the constant problem, you may want to consider switching jobs. It's a drastic move, absolutely. But remember that chronic stress can and will damage your health. However stressful switching jobs is, developing a chronic health condition is far worse. You don't have to do it overnight. Set a goal. Maybe you want to polish your resume by a certain date. Then set another goal. Maybe you want to start looking for jobs and apply to x number by x date. And then maybe you want to take a couple days off to go interview. Etc. Be methodical, using the tools you learned earlier.

Similarly, if you're living way too far from places you need to be every day, and the stress of coming and going is becoming impossible to bear, it's worth looking for a new home, even if it may be a slow process. Take it slow and steady. Don't rush into it and make things even harder on yourself. Also, don't stay in a situation where your health is going to ultimately suffer on all levels.

Or it could be that your house is just fine, but the people in that house are making things unbearable. If communication and therapy don't help at all, it may be time to look at alternative living arrangements.

Whatever your particular situation, there's always a way to minimize stress. It just requires taking time to honestly reflect on what the problem is. Some of these goals might be practicing the stress-relieving techniques provided. For example, you might decide to set a stress-relieving time-management goal such as, "I will schedule thirty minutes every Sunday for one month to plan out my activities for the following week." Finally, take into account the impact of a stress-free mental environment and take steps to ease the pressure on your overactive, stress-hormone-producing amygdalae.

All of these activities require a small time commitment, so you'll need to use time-management strategies to avoid further stress. But that time commitment is vital to your well-being and to the overall goal of this book—teaching you how to find stress relief in concrete, practical ways that are applicable to your daily life.

Chapter 8 - Relaxation Techniques For Anxiety

Relaxation is an incredibly effective way of dealing with anxiety, and it applies to all groups of people. It allows the body to activate its natural response to combat stressors. Relaxation comes in many forms and depends on what works best for you. Some of the relaxation techniques that have been proven to beat back anxiety are:

- Relaxation exercises such as muscle relaxation and deep breathing

- Meditation

- Visualization

- Physical activities like yoga

There is a common belief among many people that relaxation involves sitting idle and or doing something you enjoy, like watching a movie or sleeping. No, relaxation is a task that needs concentration and energy input. Its sole purpose is to reduce the effects of stress and anxiety. If your definition of relaxation doesn't meet this goal, then it is far from relaxation. The real meaning of that term is allowing your body to activate its natural relaxation response to bring about some balance and restore some order in your system. Relaxation achieves this by putting your body to a state of deep rest and restores normalcy such as slowing the heart rate, reducing blood pressure, improve blood circulation, and most importantly checking stress and anxiety. Activities that involve relaxation are those that touch on the most affected organs like the heart, blood vessels, and those in the breathing system. Try things like muscular exercises, meditation, yoga, and deep breathing. Most of these exercises are a form of self-treatment, so you don't need a professional to do them. However, they are quite demanding and require a lot of discipline. If you are the type that needs to be pushed, you might consider looking for a professional therapist to help you do the exercises. The word 'professional' is key because not anybody can make you do things that make you uncomfortable, especially if you're an adult. You need someone that will be hard and a little harsh on you. Also, people have diverse systems that respond differently to changes. If one or two of these exercises don't work for you, look for one that you are comfortable doing and is compatible with your system. You don't have to kill yourself trying to make a particular technique work even you can see that it is not working. Furthermore, all these techniques have been proven to lead to the same results, which is slowing down stress and anxiety. Just don't be too lazy to give a particular technique trial and error period before giving up on it entirely. Remember things take time; you need to give your body a chance to get used to these changes. You will get used to those exercises in no time, and they will become a habit.

There is a thin line between relaxation exercises and meditation exercises. The main difference being that relaxation exercises engage various parts of the physical body while meditation engages the brain. The similarity between them is that they both put the entire body and mind in a state of rest to relief affected parts and organs from stress and anxiety. Both exercises are carried out in systematic steps to the end. Skipping one step will likely jeopardize the whole process. If you are not sure about these steps and the order in which they are done, it is advisable that you seek the help of a therapist who will take you through each step.

There are various exercises that involve relaxation, as discussed below.

Deep Breathing

This is the bedrock of all other relaxation exercises. It is the simplest yet very effective way of keeping your anxiety level in check. It communicates safety to the brain, thus easing tension, stress, and anxiety. It involves improving your breathing by cleansing and opening air cavities for normal breathing to occur. Anybody can do this without any difficulty. It doesn't matter where you do it, anywhere is a perfect place as long as the environment is conducive. Conducive means it is free from noise and particle pollution. There should also be minimal disruption from other people and things. Remember this is a procedure with its own timeline; if you are interrupted say in the third step, you won't resume the exercise from the third step. You will have to start all over again and make sure it goes to completion. This is the procedure:

Identify a quiet spot outdoors, say in the park, or lock yourself up in a clean well-ventilated room. You can also sit down on a chair with your feet touching the ground or lie down with your body straight against the ground or floor. Whatever position makes you feel comfortable.

Sit up straight with your legs straight against the floor or ground, spread them apart or fold them on the knees and let the back of your feet touch. Your back should not lean on anything. Your left hand should be on your abdomen and the right on the chest. Take a deep breathe through your nose for as long as you can, relax the hand on your abdomen to allow the stomach muscles to relax and accommodate more air.

Exhale through your mouth for as long as you can, lightly push your stomach in and contract the muscles to push all the air out.

Repeat this process for like five minutes non-stop. Minimize the movement of the arm on your chest. Focus only on your breathing and try to shut down your brain from all thoughts, whether positive or negative. Make sure the breathing is slow and smooth, don't try to increase the pace. Do this thrice day, each exercise should last at least five minutes, but you can go up to fifteen minutes if you like.

Progressive Muscle Relaxation

This is a two-step process of muscular contraction and relaxation involving various groups of muscles in the body. This exercise is important because it demonstrates how your body physically responds to stress and anxiety. Remember, this is a mental disorder that is not easy to detect, but if we incorporate physical aspects in detection, it will be much easier to know when we are experiencing anxiety. The exercise can be combined with deep breathing to yield maximum results. For you to carry out this exercise, you must be in your best form health-wise; no muscle spasms, no back pains or recent injuries that might put unnecessary strain on the muscles. In case you have or suspect to have any of these problems, consult your doctor before starting the exercise. Here is the procedure.

Put on some comfortable loose clothing or loosen the ones you are wearing by unbuttoning top buttons and sleeves. Remove belts and shoes.

Repeat the steps as those in deep breathe, do it once or twice in this step.

Look at your feet in turn, start with one and spend some seconds looking at it. Move your toes slowly and follow their movement and other induced movements within the foot. Squeeze the muscles as tightly as you can within the foot. Make sure the muscles are tense for some ten seconds before relaxing them. Notice the change and difference between the two exercises.

Repeat this for the other foot and focus on the movement and behavior of the muscles as you squeeze them, and when you relax them.

Notice what tension does to your feet. You can do this by comparing how the foot feels when in tension and when relaxed.

Shift your attention to other groups in your body, such as the hand muscles, stomach muscles, and neck and shoulder muscles. Repeat the process for each and pay attention. Notice the kind feeling associated with tensing various groups of muscles.

Relaxation by Visualizing

This technique involves playing games with the brain by showing it what it desires. It is a very effective technique to combat anxiety because it gives you temporary peace and calmness. You can cultivate this good feeling by repeating this exercise for as many times as possible until it sticks.

If you feel like you're experiencing anxiety, find a quiet place, and make yourself comfortable. You can sit or stand against something like a wall.

Close your eyes, think of your ideal space — a place you would like to be in the real world or just an imaginary one.

Imagine the life there, the feeling, smell of things there, and their sounds. Think about the people you would find in that place and how awesome they are. Let that picture stick in your mind.

Open your eyes and take a deep breathe, severally. Try to feel your mind and notice if you are still experiencing anxiety.

If the anxiety tries to crawl back again, close your eyes once more and retrieve the picture of your ideal place from your mind and go back there. Experience the peace, calmness, and comfort associated with that place for as long as you can.

Repeat this process every time you feel anxious and notice if there are any changes in the completion of the exercise. Remember that the effectiveness of the procedure is determined by the amount of time you give the body to process the change. It never comes that easy, so be patient.

Relaxation through Yoga

Yoga is a workout trend that has taken the world by storm in the last ten years. It combines a series of moving and stationary poses. It also involves meditation, and this makes it an all-round relaxation technique. Apart from increasing stability, stability, and general fitness, yoga is also a powerful weapon to fight anxiety. The following different types of yoga deal with different bodily and mental problems.

Satyananda yoga- this traditional form of yoga is usually considered to be the original yoga. It is centered on meditation though it also incorporates slow poses and deep breathing. This gives it an incredible ability to combat anxiety and other psychological disorders. It is the easiest type of yoga if you are a beginner.

Hatha yoga- this type of yoga involves moderate poses and movements. After mastering all aspects of Satyananda yoga, hatha yoga is the next step to sharpen your yoga skills and improve your ability to keep anxiety at bay.

Power yoga- this is the most intense type of yoga; we can say it is a reserve of the pros. However, this intense poses gives you the ability to deal with intense stress.

Tai chi- most authors don't consider this a type of yoga, but there is a strong reason to classify it as yoga. It involves moving your body in a slow, systematic pattern and accompany it with slow but deep breathing. It is a powerful relaxation method to relieve stress and anxiety.

Like we have seen earlier, meditation is more of a psychological approach to combat anxiety. It involves freeing your mind to choose thoughts with the hope that this will serve as a counter-trigger. There are two main types of meditation.

Mindfulness Meditation

The effectiveness of this method has been put to the test by therapists, physicians, and psychologists for the last two decades. The results have been quite impressive, and it has since been used as a tool to relieve the mind from stress and anxiety. How exactly this method works is still a mystery, but it remains a powerful anxiety therapy method. Some authors have suggested that it works by confining the brain to the present, and by doing that it shuts down traumatic memories and uncertainties of the future. This makes a lot of sense because most stresses are caused by trauma and fear of what might happen. By eliminating these two, the brain can then focus only on current events. Events that deal with reality, free of perceived threats. This is how to practice mindfulness:

Repeat all the steps as with deep breathing above. Focus on your breathe alone, follow every inhalation and exhalation for as long as you can.

Monitor your mind as you focus on your breathing. Try to notice when your thoughts are about to wander and try to follow them. Notice the sounds, smells, and types of worries that your mind picks, then try to bring them back by going back to focusing on your breathing.

Allow your mind to wander once more, not anything particular, but to anything it wants. Let this wandering go on for a while then bring it back again by focusing on your breathing.

Repeat the process for about 10 minutes, twice a day or five times a week. Notice if there is any change in the level of anxiety from when you started the exercise.

Body Scan Meditation

This technique is almost similar to progressive muscle relaxation. The only difference is that it involves listening to the reaction of other parts of the body to muscular movement without judgment. This is the procedure for body scan meditation.

Lie on your back, relax your hands on your sides and keep your legs straight or crossed. Close your eyes and take a deep breathe through the nose and exhale through the mouth. Follow your breathing for like five minutes.

Shift your focus to your feet, contract the muscles of the right foot, and notice the movement of the toes. Feel the effect this tension on the muscles has on different parts of the body as you tense them even tighter.

Repeat this process for the left foot and feel the tension in other regions.

Move to a different body part, say your thighs, and repeat this process. Try noticing the impact this tension has on other parts of the body. Keep moving to your knees, calf, torso, abdomen until you have scanned every part.

After you are done, sit in stillness and quietness and try to remember what you felt in different parts and organs during the exercise.

Repeat this procedure twice or thrice a day and notice the changes in your level of anxiety.

Benefits of Relaxation Techniques

All these techniques have a wide range of benefits both to the body and to the mind. Apart from the benefit of managing anxiety, relaxation techniques are helpful in various other areas as follows:

Improved breathing- techniques that involve deep breathing like meditation and yoga play an important role in opening up air pipes and facilitating the free flow of clean air in and out of the system. Even if one experiences anxiety, chances are that their breathing system will not be harmed.

Mental stability- these exercises and techniques do not only curb anxiety, but they also prevent many other psychological and mental disorders, so you are actually killing two birds with one stone. This is made possible when you keep your mind busy and divert it from the cause of anxiety. This diversion applies to other underlying conditions of the mind.

Spices up one's social life- most of these relaxation activities and techniques are done in groups such as yoga classes and Tai chi. They expose one to different kinds of people and actually make them more sociable. Once someone starts socializing with others, the chances are that they will talk about their problems and get help.

Boosts confidence- anxiety becomes worse if the affected individual considers themselves weak. As soon as these exercises start gaining momentum, you will notice a feeling of self-pride and confidence running through you. This is a hidden benefit of applying these relaxation techniques.

Engages the brain- most people would actually use their free time to worry about ambiguous threats. This will only increase their chances of developing anxiety. Participating in these relaxation exercises will engage the brain, and you won't be thinking about some imaginary threats and problems. By the time you are done with the exercise, it will be time to resume your normal duties, and this keeps your too brain busy to indulge in unhealthy thinking.

Keep in mind that not everyone responds well to anxiety exercises and relaxation techniques. The symptoms may actually worsen for some people. If you notice that these exercises are not doing you any good, go see a doctor immediately for further direction. Seeking professional help is important since you might be suffering from other hidden illnesses.

Explanation of the Reference Technique

This is a technique that attempts to divert the mind from a perceived threat or source of anxiety by shutting down most body reflexes that receive, process, and respond to these threats. It is very effective in offering self-therapy when dealing with anxiety and other psychological disorders. The reference technique follows the following steps.

Find a comfortable and quiet place, and sit down, close your eyes.

Think of things that follow a chronological order like numbers, letters of the alphabet, months, or days. Start counting from the start to the end. Start counting again but this time in the opposite direction, from the last to the first.

Focus attention on various parts of the body as you do the counting. Notice if there is some reducing tension in some groups of muscles like those in the abdomen, back, and neck. Don't stop counting as you do the listening.

Suspend all muscular activities by turning off the muscles. Don't tense or relax them; just stay still, and focus on your counting.

Release your mind to think about anything, give it the freedom to wander from one thought to another, including your worries. Don't try and stop it if it tries to think about unpleasant things. Just listen and view the pictures without being judgmental.

After allowing your mind to wander on all kinds of thoughts, now start sorting out those thoughts. Removing all negative thoughts, those that you consider unpleasant and makes you worried. Only remain with positive thoughts and statements that make you feel safe and peaceful. Reflect on these positive thoughts for like two minutes.

Open your eyes, take a deep breath, and reflect on the feeling you have just experienced before opening your eyes.

Repeat this for some two times every day and notice whether your level of anxiety is changing from the first day.

Aromatherapy Can Help, Let's use Creativity!

I will compare this unique kind of self-therapy with an expectant woman. Some ladies are known to develop strange behaviors when pregnant. One of them is cravings. You will be surprised to learn some have the weirdest cravings. My first cousin is one such woman. When she was five months pregnant, I happened to have visited her place. Everything was okay until she woke up in the dead of night, demanding petrol. Yes, you heard that, right! She was not using a generator, nor did she have a car that uses petrol. When her husband asked her what she wants petrol for, she gave a hilarious answer that left us in stitches. She just wanted a little to sniff. When we were still treating her demand as a joke, she started behaving weirdly. She looked like she was about to have a panic attack. We had to join the village witches in that ungodly hour with a jar, walking from house to house at 4 AM. We were lucky enough to find a good neighbor who braved the morning cold and siphoned for us some from his car. We gave it to my cousin to sniff, and she became alright, almost instantly.

Aromatherapy works exactly the same way. Aromatherapy is the alternative and integrative medication used in the control of stress and anxiety. The substance used in this procedure is a natural product or products, mostly from plants, to treat anxiety. This technique has been used since long ago for this purpose; it has a commendable record of effectiveness. So why not try it too? This is how the technique is applied to treat anxiety:

·   Collect different parts of plants, preferably of the species Matricaria recutita and Lavandula ssp. These plants might not be found in your local area so you might have to buy the whole processed package.

·   Extract their oil through simple distillation. Store the oil in a clean container and make it airtight. Store the bottle in a dark space with a temperature of about -20 degrees Celsius.

·   Apply the oil to different parts of the body once a day for a period of two to three months. The method of application involves pouring some oil into your palm, rub it on the skin in any body part and spread it slowly and gently with your fingers. Massage yourself slowly for some ten minutes. You can ask someone else, preferably a therapist, to assist in the massaging.

·   Repeat this for different parts of the body every day until the two or three months are over.

·   Compared your level of anxiety at the end of the treatment and at the beginning to see if there has been any improvement.

The effectiveness of this natural technique in the treatment of anxiety has been proven by medical practitioners the world over. So, why not give it a try? Not as a last option but as a unique approach in combating anxiety. Just like my cousin, maybe you need just one touch of aromatherapy to heal your anxiety.

Chapter 9 - Be More Mindful To Escape Depression

To count your blessings, to be aware of your negative thoughts before they poison your mind, to escape depressive thoughts, and to stop thinking about past events that bring you misery, you need to live in the moment and be more mindful of yourself.

One reason why you find it difficult to forgive yourself and move on or shift your focus to the positives from the negatives is because you are not mindful of yourself and the life you have: you are forgetful of everything existing in your life.

Forgetfulness happens when you ignore your present altogether, focus on your past or future, and keep thinking of unhappy things. If you lost your job and are bankrupt now, you will not think of what you can do now to improve your situation or the lovely family by your side now. Instead, you may remain focused on why you lost your job. This is forgetfulness and this is what you need to fight to conquer depression for good.

The best way to do this is to stay mindful of yourself in each moment and do everything with full attention.

Cultivating Mindfulness in Everything You Do

Mindfulness is a state of full and deep awareness, one that makes you peaceful because you choose to focus on what you are doing and what you have instead of what was or what can be. Naturally, when your focus shifts to your present from the past or future, you become more positive, thankful, focused, and relaxed. This helps you fight depression and end it forever.

To do that, make sure to always, I repeat always, be on top of your thoughts by engaging in everything you do and doing one thing at a time. If you are walking towards the door, focus on the steps you take as well as how you move your feet. This will keep you engaged in this activity so you do not let your mind wander off in thought. If you are writing an email, speak each word loudly so you focus on the email and nothing else.

Similarly, whatever you do, pay full attention to each step of the task so you become involved in it. It will take a few tries before you perfect this strategy but once you start becoming mindful of yourself and your life, you will start enjoying and loving your life because you will seldom find yourself dwelling in the past or future.

Make sure you write how you feel after exercising this technique (and everything else taught in this book) in your journal so you can track your performance and feel proud of your accomplishments. As you become more mindful, you will start being more forgiving towards yourself too.

If you make a mistake, you will not focus on why you faltered. Instead, you will forgive yourself and make the most of your present so you can do better now and in the future. If you do not stay mindful of a task one time, you will not whine of how you were forgetful; you will choose to be more mindful now so you do not make the same mistakes again.

This improvement prompts you not to listen to the condemning and self-depreciating inner voice that keeps reminding you of your failures, mistakes, and setbacks. When the annoying voice inside you says, "You performed that terribly the last time," you will not focus on it and will instead say, "I will do it better this time around?" This shift helps you move from insanity to sanity, from sadness to happiness, and from negativity to positivity. This shift and your newfound positivity will help you live a good life.

Your job does not end here; there is one more thing you should do too: love yourself and pay more attention to your needs. Let us talk about it the following section.

Love Yourself More than Ever

Loving yourself means being there for yourself, being kind to yourself, making healthy personal decisions, prioritizing your needs first, and paying attention to yourself. Do all of this and you will start feeling amazing because you will nurture yourself and shall focus on your well-being.

Instead of paying attention to the crap people have to offer to you, you will do things that matter to you and will be more concerned about your needs. To get out of depression, loving yourself is imperative.

Let us see how you can do that.

Firstly, eliminate negative and unsupportive people in your life who keep pulling you down and always make you think negatively. If a friend bullies you or a cousin reminds you of your failures, stop meeting that friend, and instead spend time with happy people.

Secondly, do things you love doing so you can stay busy at all times. If you love basketball, play it often and with friends. If you enjoy reading, read good books whenever you are free and stay busy because staying busy is a good way to fight meaningless thoughts that shift your focus to the negatives in life.

Thirdly, start exercising more and spend more time outdoors since <u>research</u> shows exercising and spending time in nature increases production of mood enhancing hormones in your body and helps you stay fresh and active. To achieve this goal, you do not have to go to the gym every day for an hour or spend an hour in a forest. Start with baby steps and gradually make your way to bigger goals. Begin with a 5-minute exercise such as a brisk walk or doing 5 jumping jacks and slowly go for a 10 minute long walk. Once you make a habit of it, increase your exercise duration so you can reap more of its benefits.

Fourthly, identify your goals, passions, and desires and pursue them. If you ever aspired to be a singer, make time for it now and take it seriously. Following your heart's desires and goals adds meaning to your life. Setting goals also gives you an opportunity to prove yourself worthy, feel proud of yourself, and fall in love with life again.

Chapter 10 - Treatment For Depression

Treatment for depression comes in many forms. One of these treatment forms may be suitable for you. However, know that researchers are also working on new approaches to treating depression that may be better suited for you.

Drugs

Medications are a temporary cure for depression. Medications are something you can build a intolerance to. They can also cause more depression in you, depending on your body and mind.

Some individuals who have taken anti-depressants actually feel more fatigue and suicidal. Citalopram is a common anti-depressant given for depression. Reports indicate that 30% of people on this medication find they are used to it within a few months and their symptoms are no longer being taken care of. Medications can also lead to addictions and health issues. Most anti-depressants have a long list of side effects, do's and don'ts that are not good for you.

Therapy

Numerous types of therapy exist. Cognitive behavior therapy (CBT) is the most common therapy used by psychologists today. It has been effective for many people, but there are also setbacks with this type of therapy. CBT requires you to actively attempt to retrain the way you think.

In therapy and on your own, you are asked to record your negative thought. What was the situation that caused this negative thought? How did you react? What are five or more ways, you could have reacted better? The idea is that if you face the same situation again, you are able to think of a more positive response and use it. It is also a therapy, where you are asked to slow down and assess the situation.

If you stop, think, listen, correct your internal reaction, then you are able to gain a better overall reaction in various situations. Let's assess an example.

Say you are at work. You made a mistake. You are in a depressive state. You call yourself stupid, you say it aloud to others, and you are unhappy the rest of the day.

In therapy, you would be asked to stop, think about those thoughts, and listen to how harmful they are. You would then need to determine how you could have reacted better, such as saying "I made a mistake. It does not make me less of a person, but I do need to learn from this mistake, and try to avoid it in the future."

In this way, you acknowledge the problem, you accept that mistakes happen because people are not perfect, and you will learn from it in the future.

Therapy can also be one-on-one sessions, where you talk about your feelings. Sometimes you just need to talk, to unload, and you are able to see things clearly. It is not complaining or useless time, as long as the person helping you works with depression. You want someone who is an expert in depression versus a common therapist or counselor, particularly if you have severe depression.

Support Groups

Support groups should be used in conjunction with therapy. Support groups provide you with a place to go and talk about your troubles, with others who share the same troubles. Seeing that others are in difficult situations and depressed can help you reflect on your own behavior.

Changing Relationships

Not all relationships are healthy for you. Some relationships enable you to continue being depressed. Other relationships are not giving you what you need, such as support and attention. Changing these relationships can help you find your self-worth and get on the path to recovery.

Herbal Remedies

St. John's Wart is just one herb known to help with depression on a short-term basis. There are also teas with herbs in them that are known to help with depression because they help calm you and correct hormonal imbalances. Herbs are not always the answer and should not be taken unless you speak with a physician or mental health professional first.

Chapter 11 - New Approaches And Methods To Treat Depression

Researchers are consistently looking for ways to treat depression. There is not a specific cure all for depression. Some treatments work for certain patients, but not to others. To a degree, researchers are still asking questions about why depression occurs. Yes, there are certainly specific causes depression has been linked to; however, there some individuals that find no help in current treatments.

There are still unanswered questions about the hereditary properties of depression in certain family groups. All of these unanswered questions are leading researchers towards new methods of treatment, with the aim of treating more patients successfully.

One new approach to depression has targeted brain dysfunctions, cognitive, and emotional processes, which trigger depression symptoms. Greg J. Siegle is the director of the Program in Cognitive Affective Neuroscience, located at the University of Pittsburgh School of Medicine. Dr. Siegle states their new approach is to think of the brain as a muscle, which has atrophied, like the heart muscle atrophies during a stroke. He believes the brain is a muscle that needs to be rehabbed.

Their efforts have been to study the effects of computer games, math problems, and audio chirping birds to stimulate the emotional regulation of the brain. Other researchers use words and faces to help depressed individuals to disengage from the negative stimuli and focus on positive stimuli.

Computer games are used along with electrical stimulation of the brain in some studies. These treatments have mixed results. Scientists are working to determine the appropriate doses and they know that this therapy protocol will not work for all patients. The concept behind the new approach is to try something for individuals that have certain brain dysfunction leading to depression.

Scientists have taken images of depressed brains to try to map the areas of the brain affected by the disorder. They are working on treatments that target these areas in an attempt to "heal" the brain (Petersen, 2015).

Cognitive Control Training

Dr. Siegle is just one of the professionals working on depression treatments, who believe old therapies are not offering the greatest help possible. Simon Rego is the director of psychology training located at the Montefiore Medical Center in New York. Dr. Rego believes cognitive behavioral therapy or CBT is too hard for people suffering from depression. CBT is a retraining of the brain to stop thinking negatively, by analyzing the situation, your reaction, and coming up with positive ways to assess the emotions.

Dr. Rego feels people who are depressed have low energy, motivation, and concentration. It is difficult for a therapy to ask for a task to be completed that is opposite of what one's energy level is.

CCT is his alternative suggestion. With Cognitive Control Training, a person suffering from depression is asked to perform two exercises that last 15 minutes each. The patients are given numbers that are in a series. These numbers have set rules. The task is an attempt to activate an area of the prefrontal cortex called the dorsal lateral. It is the part of the brain associated with emotion regulation, as well as executive control. Dr. Siegle states it is an area that "voluntarily thinks" about something when you want it to. Dr. Siegle is part of the team that has developed CCT. He believes this underactive area of the brain is why many people ruminate on negative thoughts, which plague them, and make them feel depressed.

CCT includes listening to the sounds of birds chirping. These external sounds culminated with active and direct attention on the sounds, allows a person to concentrate on something other than their own thoughts.

The report, published in Behavioral and Cognitive Psychotherapy discussed a study that involved 48 people. These people suffered from depression. They were given three sessions of CCT. These sessions occurred in a two-week period. The depression scores dropped more significantly, than people obtaining CBT control exercises. The study was published in 2014.

A group located in Australia has also examined CCT with trans cranial direct current stimulation (tDCS). An electric current, on a gentle setting, is used while video games are played. A study called Brain Stimulation was published in 2014 based on this study. It showed depressed patients who had a combination of CCT and electrical stimulation experienced a 46% reduction in their symptoms after three weeks of treatment. Individuals who received only CCT saw a decrease in symptoms of only 17% and those with electrical stimulation only saw an 8.9% reduction.

Among the new therapies developed, Dr. Siegle has worked on exercises in concentration. He uses two electrodes on the arm, passing a very weak current through the body. The placement of the electrode causes an itching sensation that is extremely annoying. Patients find it difficult to think negative thoughts with this itching occurring (Petersen, 2015).

Interpretation Bias Modification

Interpretation Bias Modification is also called Cognitive Bias Modification-Interpretation (CBM-I). It is a new treatment Dr. Jamie Micco, at Harvard Medical School has been working on.

Micco is an assistant professor. He stated CBM-I tries to contradict the way people look at ambiguous situations and then react negatively.

In one study, he had patients look at written scenarios. These scenarios were positively resolved, but often the last word was missing a letter and patients needed to fill it in. CBM-I's goal is to help patients think in a positive or neutral way, versus the negative their brain's focus on.

Further testing for CBM-I treatment has people look at two faces, one neutral in expression and the other sad. The patient is trained to look away from the negative and focus on the neutral, just as the patient is asked to focus on neutral words versus negative words.

The Journal of Abnormal Psychology published a study in 2015 relating to CBM as a way to reduce negative focus. The treatment contained a placebo, where 52 subjects were studied for four weeks. Patients noticed a 40% reduction in symptoms. The study's authors thought the placebo treatment actually enhanced the attention of patients, which helped reduce the symptoms patients felt.

The new approaches discussed focus mainly on the negative attention depressed patients have. They are biased towards negative thoughts versus positive thoughts. About 2/3 thirds of patients with depression have these rumination troubles, and the other third do not. It is very important for a trained professional to treat a patient with depression based on their symptoms, reactions to situations, and physical well-being. To be successful one has to understand the neurobiological and cognitive issue in the patient, so that treatment can be designed specifically for the patient (Petersen, 2015).

Treatment-Resistant Depression Approaches

Neuromodulation is one type of treatment patients are incorporating into their depression treatment, when all other methods have failed. It is designed to pass electrical current through the brain.

There are a couple of types of this treatment: electroconvulsive therapy, Vagus nerve stimulation and repetitive transcranial magnetic stimulation. These all use a type of weak electrical current that is transmitted by the electrodes. They work on stimulating specific areas of the brain, such as the Vagus nerve (University of Michigan, 2016).

The Vagus nerve supplies the lungs, heart, upper digestive tract and other organs. It is a cranial nerve that provides parasympathetic control of these organs. Research studies indicate stimulating these organs and the nerve can relieve pain, but also help a person retrain their brain to think in a more positive manner. It is also a nerve that Psychology Today links with "gut instincts."

A study in Switzerland found the nerve provides feelings, what we call gut instincts to the brain. These are the instinctual feelings that tell us when there is danger or when we have the right answer. By using electrical current, the nerve is stimulated to feel less "threatening" feelings, thus allowing happier thoughts to enter the brain.

This and the other treatments discussed are in early testing. Only small groups of people have been tested. As new approaches, these treatments are seemingly positive for certain types of patients.

If you have tried other treatments, without success or feel that CBT is too much work for your current depressive state, you may wish to find a study near you or ask your current physician/therapist about these options.

The more information you gather about potential help with your depression, the more comfortable and in control you will start to feel. Depending on the severity of your depression, a small step of gaining control can push you towards a more energetic reaction. It could provide you with the desire needed to get your brain engaged, actively, in treating your depression versus losing interest or concentration again and again.

When one therapy does not work, do not give up. You just have not found the right therapy for you. It does exist, but it also takes work and the driving need to want the help.

Chapter 12 - How To Find Fulfillment In Life

You can begin your own treatment. If you have sought a diagnosis from a physician or psychologist, you can work towards a treatment plan with them, as well as with yourself. Depression has many causes, but among them and often the most prevalent is feeling worthless, stupid, and low self-esteem. This cycle of emotions can be broken. These steps may not work for everyone. You may have tried them and found no success, but perhaps it was your self-discipline and approach.

The Mind is a Powerful Organ

Your mind is extremely powerful. It is the epicenter of your entire life. Without your brain, you would be an empty shell. The phrase "you cannot teach an old dog new tricks," is a myth. Worse, it is wrong. You can teach your aging brain new tricks. You can change how it reacts, thinks, and processes information. All you need to do is be willing and discover any underlying factors that might hinder this process.

Here are some things that may make these steps difficult:

You have an illness, you do not know about, thyroid disorder, beginnings of dementia, or other hormonal imbalance.

You suffer from a chemical imbalance.

Your brain may not be connected properly via the nervous system.

Genetic causes might be affecting your brain process.

You are in the middle of a great loss, which is making your depression worse.

You have PTSD (post-traumatic stress disorder) that is leading to depression.

Make absolutely certain that your depression is not a result of a biological condition. Also, assess the rest of your life to determine if PTSD, abuse, or a death in your immediate family/friends circle is making your depression worse. Armed with the best list of causes for your depression, means you are armed to correct all aspects of the depression, as well as gain fulfillment from life.

Your Treatment Plan

Beginning with the understanding of your depressions cause, you can now work on a self-treatment plan to find joy in life.

Get a journal or start one on your computer.

Keep this journal with you at all times.

On the first page, write out 1 positive feeling about yourself. It may be that you love your hair color, its length, or your eyes.

You might write that you love the strength you have in difficult situations. No matter what it is, it needs to be a compliment.

Underneath this compliment, write 1 goal for your life. This goal can be obtaining a new job, going back to school, finishing school, travelling somewhere. The only caveat is the goal has to be something you can accomplish, realistically.

 If it is a goal, such as going back to school, then your job is to take small steps towards this long term goal. It can also be a short term goal. You might set a goal about waking up, lying in bed for 10 minutes, and thinking only of positive thoughts. Whatever goal you set, you need to be able to make it.

The next task is to create a meaning of life chart, diagram, map, or list. This is not about goals. It is about what would make life more meaningful to you. The Buddhists believe that the end to suffering is to forgo the materialistic things and desires we have. If you desire love and you have been unable to attain it, then you may feel depressed. So what are the things that have greater meaning?

How to see the Greater Meaning

When in the throes of depression, it is difficult, nearly impossible to see the greater meaning to your life. You tend to feel worthless versus meaningful. However, all is not lost.

Writing out your emotions is the best way to find what is most meaningful to you. A person lost her father. Her father was a friend and a mentor, as well as a loved one.

Instead, of being sad and angry at the loss, she focused on the meaning he gave to her life, the happy moments that they shared together. She did not forget about the times when they argued when she was growing up, but instead, remembered the lessons from those times.

She also had the most important lesson he gave to her and that was, "I have lived my life with no regrets." Her father taught her that all mistakes, disappointments, and happiness in life is where the meaning of life comes from. It is not about dwelling on the bad, on the things that cannot be changed, but the focus should be on the positive that was gained from any situation.

Those words held more power in getting over her depression and sense of loss than any others. Perhaps they can for you as well. Take time now to consider what has happened in your life that was good.

Was there a time you felt worthwhile? Was there a person who made you feel worthy and important? If you can find one happy memory, then you can start to recall the others. From this, you can discover true meaning in your life.

Most of us do not want to feel like our existence is for naught. Yet, we also know that life ends. You are born, you live, and you die. In death, the only thing that could bring meaning to your life is how you are remembered. For some, it is about accomplishing great feats—perhaps writing the great American novel. For others, it is the family they have, the lessons they have left behind, and the community influence they have provided.

You are not going to find the meaning in your life immediately. It can take a week, a month, a year, or several years. The point is not rushing to a solution about your depression and finding fulfillment immediately, but about the trip it takes you to get there. It is also about the changes you make, so you can get to a point of realizing what fulfillment truly means.

Chapter 13 - 8 Simple Exercises

Do physical activity

The definition of physical activity in this context has not been limited only to exercise. Physical activity is any activity that engages your physique. Mostly it will lead to perspiration. When an individual engages in physical activity, he or she is obliged to concentrate fully on that particular activity. Exercising is a very renowned way to counter depression. Regular exercise has time and again been used as an anti-depressant. When one is exercising, endorphins are boosted. These are chemicals that enable an individual to feel good.

The statistics of how many people deal with stress is always on the upward. When one experiences stress, it has a lasting effect in their lives since it cuts across what an individual is engaging in at a particular time. To eradicate stress completely is an uphill task, and one would rather manage it. Exercising is one of the best methods to manage stress. Many medical practitioners advise that individuals should engage in exercises in a bid to manage stress levels.

The advantages that come with a person engaging in exercises have far been established to be a counter-measure against diseases and as a method of enhancing the body's physical state. Research has it that exercising helps a great deal when decreasing fatigue and enhancing the body's consciousness to the environment. Stress invades the whole of your body, affecting both the body and mind. When this happens, the act of your mind feeling well will be pegged on the act of the body feeling well too. When one is in the act of exercising, the brain produces endorphins which act naturally as pain relievers. They also improve the instances upon which an individual falls asleep. When the body is able to rest, this means that its amounts of anxiety have dropped by a large margin. Production of endorphins can also be triggered by the following practices. They include but are not limited to meditation and breathing deeply. Participation in exercise regularly has proven an overall tension reliever.

Doing relaxation exercises

Another method of reducing stress levels is through the use of some relaxation techniques. A relaxation technique is any procedure that is of aid to an individual when trying to calm down the levels of anxiety. Stress is effectively conquered when the body itself is responding naturally to the stress levels in the body. Relaxation can be often confused with laying on a couch after a hard day. This relaxation is best done in the form of self-meditation, although its effects are not fulfilling on the impact of stress. Most relaxation techniques are done at the convenience of your home with only an app.

Settling on the right technique for relieving stress is not easy. It is key that you focus on one that is not only favorable to your lifestyle but also your budget. There are various techniques for mind relaxation, which are:

Deep breathing

When breathing deeply, one increases the neuron-transmitters known as endorphins that seek to bring about a feeling of easiness. This technique forms the basis for other types of techniques. In order to achieve this, one needs to sit in a posture that allows his or her back to be straight. One hand should be firmly placed on the chest and the other on the stomach. An individual should inhale through the nostrils and exhale through the mouth. This procedure should be carried out cyclically and repetitive.

Continuous muscle relaxation

This happens in a two-phase kind of arrangement in that there are the contraction and relaxation of muscles. One phase entails tensing the muscles while the other involves relaxing them. This type of stress reliever works best when you ascend all the way up from your legs. Normally you should have lost clothing on with no shoes. You should take your time to practice the shifts in breathing. Commence with your right foot then your left making sure that you feel every moment of it. The movement should be in ascension, making sure you touch every muscle in your body.

Meditation

While in the process of meditation, make sure that you go through your whole body in your mind.

This will automatically assume an ascension kind of manner. Make sure that you face upwards with your legs separated. Focus on every particular part of your body, taking note of the different reactions that you are feeling. After going through your body, take some time to relax in a mode of doing nothing.

Vision of peace

Our eyes need to be shut during this particular exercise. Here, you close your eyes and see yourself in a state that is devoid of any technicalities. You need to see yourself in a place where you are enjoying yourself to the fullest. Experience peace at its peak. Enjoy the surrounding, for instance, the clean air, the warm sun rays, the friendly water. Feel as your anxiety drifts away, leaving you at peace. After that, you can then open your eyes gently and come back to real facts.

Calculated movements

Like meditation, exercising the mind through calculated movements entails engaging the mind on the events of the present. Whereas meditation focuses on the past, exercising the mind is akin to the current situations. Take, for instance, yoga or the famous Tai chi. These movements are done in a synchronized manner, one that enables the mind to relax. When the mind is relaxing, levels of stress fall.

Write

Writing is one of the many solutions to stress relief. Writing helps reduce stress levels to individuals with anxiety disorders since jotting down your horrible experiences is one way of parting with them completely. The type of writing that focuses on the previous events that might have taken place in the life of a person is referred to as writing in the form of expression. This is because the writer is trying to connect with the readers through opening up to them, telling them what he or she has been through. This type of writing may not be effective for every individual. Some individuals may be inclined to be haunted over and over again by what they are writing. This may cause more harm than good. With writing, one tends to evaluate the situation in different ways despite the outcome.

Apart from writing as a form of expression, there is another form of writing which entails that you write from a reflective point of view. With this type of view, an individual is able to visualize the situation differently. With this kind of writing, the writer is able to unearth various things that he or she had not put into consideration. With writing, it can be so confidential that an individual is able to write what he or she is ashamed of saying out to other people. People who write about particular events in their lives are the ones that spearhead the solution process.

Managing time in the right way for you

Here stress levels are brought about by timelines that we seek to meet in order to fulfill our obligations. All around the world, we are defined by the various responsibilities that are tied to us by the inherent nature of existence. Some of us are parents, and at the same time, have demanding jobs in a bid to make ends meet. Juggling between being a parent and being apt at your place of work is not an easy task. It will always leave you worn out if not stressed.

The old saying that time is money has never been side-shadowed at any ounce. The kind of life that an individual is leading will always be defined by the kind of life that a particular individual is leading. How best an individual manages time determines the degree of how best an individual leads his or her life. For instance, it is common sense that the body needs to rest in order to rejuvenate. To do this, the body requires at least eight hours to seven hours of sleep.

Meditate

This refers to a state of relating to your conscience. Meditation happens in your mind. These are usually episodes whereby one takes time to visualize what is happening in his or her life and trying to influence it positively. Meditation acts as a stress reliever since it influences the secretion of a neuron-transmitter known as endorphin that has a calming effect on the body.

Spend time with animals

Research has it that interacting with pets, or friendly animals have a calming effect on the levels of stress that an individual has. Research has it that most mental illnesses have been curbed by pets. Co-habiting with a pet comes with a bag of goodies that include uncompromised companionship. A pet will always be there by your side even when you are feeling lonely; the feeling will be eradicated.

Pets have time and again been used as a means of getting to know each other and making friends. With a pet in place, you are inclined to form social networks that will help you connect with other people regularly. With pets around, one's blood pressure is reduced to manageable levels; your overall cardiovascular health is improved. With a pet running here and there, we will always be obliged to exercise often when playing with them. When interacting with a pet, you feel like you are having a conversation with a normal human being. This, in turn, has two effects. First is that we will not experience loneliness. We will also be inclined to forget about the worse thoughts rather than dwelling on them.

Stay in the open air

The breathing of fresh air has a lot of positive effects on our bodies. Our bodies depend on the process of breathing in order to live progressively. Having a feel of clean air or a sensation of petals aids in the alleviation of stress. The levels of serotonin produced in the body are affected by the amounts of oxygen in the body. A higher level of serotonin leads to a hyped feeling of being amazed. For instance, the sensation found in lavender aids in the reduction of insomnia. Jasmine plant, on the other hand, has been used as a boost to mood.

Research has it that failure of exposure to clean air can be a cause of death. This was after a report was released with individuals succumbing to death due to polluted air. Fresh air enhances strength in the body. The respiration process that occurs in the production of energy has it that oxygen is a raw material. Fatigue comes as a result of not being exposed to fresh air for long periods of time.

Digestion is also a key aspect when it comes to fresh air. Taking a stroll allows the body to engage in a series of reactions that will enhance the digestion to take place faster. This is opposed to the habit of eating at your office desk as you continue with your task. The digestion here is curtailed, and thus, it affects the concentration levels of a particular individual. This person is obliged not to function for a longer period without getting fatigued.

The open-air exposes our lungs to fresh air. Smoking darkens our lungs and puts us at danger of cancer. The sensation of clean air in our lungs is relieving in the sense that you are feeling every part of your air sacks. This also aids in the eradication of sputum from our chests that will, in turn, lead to blockages.

Research has it that exposure to clean air provides the requisite bacteria that is responsible for fighting off germs that cause diseases. Germs are often the causative agents of various diseases. Fresh air in eradicating this germs, maintains the status core of the body keeping you healthy. The combination of freshwater with clean air incomparable. With this in place, your stress levels will drop subsequently.

Conclusion

Having confidence is about being able to put one step in front of the last without doubting that step. It's about knowing that what you do in your life is your choice and knowing that no one else can make those choices for you. Don't live by other people's standards. Create your own.

The most important thing that you can take with you from this book is the following, which is based on a practice called mindfulness:

Yesterday is gone – You cannot change it and it doesn't count any more.

Tomorrow has not yet arrived – worrying about it won't help it to be better.

This moment in life is all that you have.

It's perfectly astute and correct to assume that this moment within your life may be all that you have. Thus, learn to embrace it and stop feeling bogged down by other people's judgment of you. If you made mistakes in the past, don't make them in this moment and don't waste this moment by letting your thoughts drag you into the past. If you can make things right with people by apologizing, do so. If you can't, learn from the mistake and don't make it again.

Depression can go away, but you have to understand that a thought that you have today isn't' important in the overall picture of life. If you waste this moment on negative thoughts, you go into the next moment with negativity already there in your life. If you fill this moment with a positive action, you reinforce your value and you move forward into the next moment as a better person than you were a moment ago. Thus, it follows that building up your confidence should be done moment by moment. I made a friend a cup of coffee because I knew that she was lonely. It made her feel better. It made me feel better. Small gestures that take selfish thought out of the picture help to build up positivity that helps to pull you out of the pits of depression. I helped a lady with her shopping because she was older and struggling. When you give, give with no expectations of return because that's the kind of giving that helps you to build up your confidence in yourself. You do things because you know they are positive things to do. You don't do them for thanks or for something given in return. When you incorporate giving into your everyday life, it's a positive reminder to yourself that you have value.

Even after a great loss in your life, you need to feel that value explained above. You may lose your purpose for a while, but if you make this your aim in life, you begin to feel you are building strong roots that will take you through all the pitfalls of life with your head held high, knowing that your personal strength and roots will help you through the bad times that come into your life. Depression is a phase. It's a stopping point to reassess who you are and make yourself even stronger and more confident, taking you back up the path to happiness.